LANTERN LANE

BOOK 2

WRITTEN BY
TESSA GREENE

COVER ILLUSTRATION BY
KRISTINA KISTER

TABLE OF CONTENTS

CHAPTER 1

Letty shivered from both excitement and the chilly dusk air. Tiny flames glimmered around her as she watched the lantern lighters igniting the final lights at the far end of Lantern Lane. Although she had only been gone for a little over a week, it felt like an eternity since Letty had been home. Perhaps it was because the castle felt so different from her own home, or maybe it was because so much of her life felt like it had flipped upside down within that time. Whatever the reason, it didn't matter much now as she stared at her father's dry goods store and her family's home directly above it. The shop's shutters were closed, but flickering candlelight filtered through the cracks: someone was still inside tidying up from the day's business.

Letty took a deep breath. Her heart fluttered as she wondered how her mother and brother would react to seeing her. If only her father were there as well, instead of being lost who-knew-where as he had been for nearly three weeks now. Letty shook her head to clear it. *Focus on the positive*, she told herself. *I'll see Papa again soon.* She wasn't entirely sure that was true anymore, but last she had heard, the search parties were still out looking, and there was still hope. That thought made her feel just a bit better.

She stepped slowly onto the porch and put her face up to the window in the front door, trying to peer through the shutters. Just as she expected, there was Miles, his back turned to the door, with a crutch under one arm as he tried to maneuver a broom with the other.

Letty grasped the doorknob, not taking her eyes off her brother. The door was unlocked. Letty wasn't surprised; it always was. A little bell above the door jingled as she entered.

"Sorry, we're closed for the night!" Miles called over his shoulder without turning around.

Letty didn't respond. A lump had suddenly formed in her throat, and although she opened her mouth, no words came out. She simply stood in the doorway.

After a moment Miles seemed to notice that the bell hadn't rung a second time to announce that the door had closed. He turned to look over his shoulder. "Is there something I can help—" he started to ask, but he fell silent the moment he saw Letty standing there. His broom clattered to the ground. "Letty," Miles whispered.

Tears began to pool in Letty's eyes as she smiled at her brother. "Hi," she breathed, barely able to form the word.

Miles raced across the room, accompanied by loud scraping and thudding sounds as he hobbled on only one crutch. Letty found herself suddenly engulfed in the biggest, tightest hug she had ever felt in her life.

"Mama! Mama, come quick!" Miles shouted up the stairs as he squeezed Letty.

Scuttling noises came through the floorboards as their mother began moving around upstairs.

"Miles! Are you all right? I thought I heard crashing noises. Did you hurt yourself?" their mother called as she hurried down the stairs. She stopped in her tracks at the bottom when she saw Miles hugging Letty. "Oh, Letty, honey," she cried, flying across the room to join Miles and Letty's hug.

Letty's tears spilled over as her mother and brother embraced her. Mama was crying too. Even Miles sniffled a bit as the three stood there holding one another.

"What are you doing here?" Mama asked at last. "Did you run away? I thought you were going to stay until we could fix things with the princess. You might get in trouble—"

Letty laughed, wiping at her eyes. "No, Mama, Princess Maisy let me come home. She knows that she made a mistake. I have so much to tell you."

"Well, come upstairs then," said Mama, breaking away from the hug and pulling Letty toward the stairs. "The stew should be just about ready now, and you can tell us all about it while we eat."

Letty allowed herself to be guided up the stairs. When she was halfway up, she heard a grunt and a scraping noise. "Hold on, I'll be right there!" Miles called.

"Oh goodness, Miles," Letty laughed, running back down the stairs to take Miles's second crutch back to him.

"Thanks," Miles said, situating the crutch under his free arm. "It's good to have you back, Letty."

Once they were settled at the kitchen table with stew and thick slices of bread in front of them, Miles and Mama listened raptly as Letty explained exactly what had happened.

"Were you frightened?" Miles asked.

"You have no idea," Letty said with a chuckle. She was able to smile about it now that she was looking back. "I was terrified, especially because the princess refused to believe that I wasn't who she thought I was, and I didn't understand why. She expected me to know exactly what she needed me to do and how to do it, and she was furious that I didn't."

"How did you manage that, Letty?" queried Mama.

"I don't think I could have on my own, but after I met Jocelyn—maybe Miles already told you about her—she and the other servants at the castle helped me write out a schedule to follow. After a bit, I learned how Princess Maisy liked things to be done."

"And she was pleased with you then?" Mama asked.

"Oh, no, not at all. She found every little thing she could to get upset about, including the dress I was wearing, but after I read your letter, Mama, I got better at standing up for myself. Princess Maisy still had her mood swings, but for the most part, it was better." Letty paused for a moment and dunked her slice of bread in her stew. The food at the castle was excellent, but she had dearly missed her mother's cooking. "It didn't get really terrible again until our fight this afternoon."

Miles cocked an eyebrow. "A fight today? What happened?"

"Well, the princess had hired a seamstress to make some new gowns because the prince of Pelorias is coming to visit. Today, they were all ready for her to try on, except she wasn't pleased with them. She threw a fit and screamed at everyone in the room, and I scolded her for being disrespectful." Letty blushed slightly. "I probably should have been more tactful."

"Who needs tact? It sounds like you did the right thing," said Miles, his eyes glowing with pride. Letty knew that Miles wouldn't have expected her to stand up for herself as she had done. She also knew that he always wished she would.

"You can try to do the right thing in the wrong way, Miles,"

Mama chided. "I'm not saying you did it in the wrong way, Letty, but I'm proud of you for taking responsibility for any mistakes you think you've made."

"Fine, fine," Miles relented with a wave of his hand. "But I still don't understand. After all that, you're going back?"

"Yes," Letty replied, "early tomorrow morning."

"Why? That princess was horrible to you. I ought to march down to the castle and give her a piece of my mind." Miles gritted his teeth and looked out the window.

Letty could practically see the hypothetical scene she was sure was playing out in his head. "We reconciled. I apologized, and so did she. She promised that she would do better—that was a big part of why I agreed to stay once Princess Maisy realized I wasn't the runaway lady-in-waiting. And besides, she needs me. It feels like the right thing to do."

Mama put her hand on Miles's arm before he could protest again. "Won't the princess need you tonight?" she asked gently.

"No. Jocelyn offered to help her get ready for bed tonight so that I could stay here longer."

"Jocelyn—you mentioned her before," Miles said. "Is she your friend who was at the window with you when Peter and I visited?"

"Yes. She's wonderful. She was the first one to realize that I wasn't the real lady-in-waiting."

"She seemed very kind," Miles responded. One side of his mouth turned up in a timid kind of smile, but Letty didn't think much of it.

"I'm glad you've found a friend," Mama said. "And if it feels like the right thing to do, we trust you."

The family ate together for a while in contented silence, grateful

5

to be together again and feel one another's presence.

When they were finished with their supper, Letty helped Mama gather the dishes and place them in the washbasin.

"Is there any news from the search parties?" Letty asked as she scrubbed at a stubborn spot on one of the bowls in the basin.

Miles and Mama looked at one another out of the corners of their eyes.

"There is," Mama said slowly. "There's a group going out all day tomorrow. Most of them are closing their businesses for the day to join."

Mama prodded at the fire, trying to maintain its warmth. She stared intently into the fire as she stoked it, and Miles gazed down at his fidgeting hands on the table. Letty looked back and forth between them. Something about their demeanor troubled her; they weren't telling her everything.

"What is it?" Letty asked. "I feel like I'm missing something here. Will someone please tell me what's going on?"

Miles sighed. "Listen, Letty," he said. "There is a group going out tomorrow like Mama said, but . . . they're the last ones. If they don't find him, they're calling off the search."

"Calling off the search?" Letty repeated. She felt like she had been punched in the stomach as the air left her lungs. Why would they call off the search? Surely they wouldn't just give up, would they? Everyone on Lantern Lane and in the surrounding village loved her father. Letty hadn't imagined the search coming to an end until her father had been found, and now she was forced to reconsider.

"They've looked everywhere they can, honey," Mama said. "There's one last section of the mountainside they're going to be covering, but besides that, they've searched the entire mountain, including on the Pelorias side. They even searched the edges of the forest as deep as they could go before it got dangerous." She pursed her lips, trying to fight back tears. "He isn't there, Letty. There's nothing more to do."

Letty's mouth gaped open. Was this really it?

"But hey, hey." Miles leaned on the table for support as he hopped to the other side to put his arm around Letty. "There's still hope. The area they're going to cover tomorrow is pretty large, and nearly every man on Lantern Lane and many more from the village will be out there. I think they can find him. I really do."

Letty breathed in deeply, releasing her breath slowly to calm herself. "You're right," she said. "We can't give up hope yet. He's out there, and they'll find him."

"Remember the search party along with your father in your prayers tonight," Mama said gently. "Now, let's finish up these dishes and get to bed. I think we've all had a very long day."

"You said you need to get back to the castle early tomorrow, right, Letty?" Miles asked. "I can take you."

"On your crutches?" asked Mama, lifting one eyebrow.

"I can manage," said Miles, "and Letty can help me if I need it."

"Not on the way back," Letty pointed out.

"Then we'll pick up Peter along the way, and *he* can help me get home," Miles countered. "He's always up early. I'm sure he'd like to join us."

"It's really all right, Miles. We don't have to bother Peter. I walked here on my own, so I'll be fine going back—"

"I'm walking you back to the castle, and that's that," Miles said firmly but with a smile.

"All right, then, it's settled," Mama said. "Let's get the two of you to bed so you have plenty of sleep before you're off again in the morning."

CHAPTER 2

A light dusting of snow coated the ground the next morning, illuminated only by the lantern light as the Kingdom of Trielle prepared to meet the sunrise.

Letty huddled into her shawl as she walked alongside Miles and Peter toward the castle. Peter had been surprised when Miles and Letty had appeared at his doorstep that morning, but Miles was right: Peter was happy to join them and eager to hear Letty's story, which she spent most of the walk telling him.

"You know," Peter said after Letty was done recounting her adventures at the castle so far, "I'm going out with the last search party today."

"Are you?" Letty asked. "When are you leaving?"

"We're meeting in front of your father's shop just after sunrise. I feel optimistic about it. We have a very careful plan laid out for exactly how and where we are going to look for him. I really think we might find him today."

"I hope you're right," Letty said. Miles nodded in agreement.

By this time they had nearly arrived at the castle. Gentle rays of sunlight were just starting to ease their way over the mountains, tinging the dark sky with gold and turning the wispy clouds overhead a soft, rosy pink.

"Letty," Miles said as they approached the castle doors, "are you sure you want to go back? We can turn around right now and go home."

"He's right," Peter added. "You don't have to do this if you don't want to."

"I know," Letty sighed, "but I *do* want to. I want to help Princess Maisy get ready for the prince to come from Pelorias. I'm excited. Now that I can visit, I'll be home again soon, and you can visit me too. So, yes, I'm sure."

"All right, then," Miles said. "I'll stop by after the search party gets back and let you know how it goes. Hopefully I'll be bringing Papa with me."

Letty gave them each a quick hug before turning toward the castle.

"Good morning," she said to one of the guards at the door. His face was familiar. She was quite sure that he was one of the guards who had brought Isla, the princess's former lady-in-waiting, back to the castle the day before.

"Ah, if it isn't the princess's new lady-in-waiting," he said. "That was quite the stand you took yesterday. I was stunned that she agreed to your conditions; you must be doing something right."

"Thank you," Letty said with a smile. The guards opened the heavy castle doors to let her inside. Letty turned back to wave to Miles and Peter one last time before stepping out of the chilly morning air and into the warmth of the grand entry.

As excited as Letty was as she made her way to the princess's chambers, she couldn't help but wonder whether this was really going to be the fresh start she was hoping for. How committed was Princess Maisy to practicing kindness and respect? Letty thought the princess would keep her promise, but she couldn't be entirely sure.

Seven gentle chimes rang through the castle as Letty reached the top of the stairs. She was just in time to wake the princess and help her prepare for the day. She took a deep breath before she entered the room, hoping for the best but preparing herself for the worst-case scenario.

Letty's worries subsided as she went through the usual morning preparations. When she tied the laces on the princess's dress, Letty could tell that something was bothering Princess Maisy. Letty grimaced, afraid that the princess would snap, but instead, Princess Maisy took a deep breath and calmly asked if Letty would please pull the laces tighter. When Letty accidentally tugged too hard on her first brush through the princess's hair, Princess Maisy politely asked Letty to be gentler, rather than insulting her competence as she often had in the past.

"How was your visit with your family?" Princess Maisy queried, shifting in her seat. Her voice was awkward and slightly strained as she spoke, as though unsure exactly how to make this sort of small talk.

"It was wonderful. Seeing Miles and my mother again was lovely. Thank you so much for letting me go."

"Is there any news about your father?" the princess asked, skipping over Letty's thanks.

"The final search party is going out today," Letty said, concentrating on the way she brushed the princess's hair so she didn't have to think too hard about the words leaving her mouth. "They're very optimistic about finding him."

Princess Maisy paused for a moment before asking, "And what if they don't?"

Letty paused now, too, unsure what to say or even what to

think. At last, she responded, "They will."

Princess Maisy only nodded, and Letty was grateful that she didn't try to push the subject further.

That morning was the best Letty had had so far in the castle. As worried as she was about her father, she managed to push her concerns to the back of her mind for the time being. After all, what good was it to worry when the search party was out looking so hard? Instead, she kept her focus on accomplishing whatever tasks Princess Maisy needed completed. She kept a wary eye out for any change in Princess Maisy's pleasant demeanor but was glad to find that there really wasn't one. Princess Maisy remained mildly awkward as she navigated polite conversation and endeavored to give kind, respectful instructions to Letty and the other servants she came across.

By the time Letty went to join Princess Maisy in the gardens for tea, a cheerful optimism had settled firmly within her. As she always did, she plucked a winter rose from the bush near the castle wall as she strolled to the spot where she and the princess would have their afternoon tea. Although she didn't feel so distant from Lantern Lane now that she was free to visit, she still loved tucking the winter rose into her pocket as a reminder of her home and the people there that she loved. As her fingers brushed across the velvety petals, she made a mental note to visit her little friends Liam and Elsie the next time she was on Lantern Lane; they would love to hear that she picked flowers to remind her of them.

A moment later, she joined Princess Maisy at the small table under a tree in the center of the gardens. After Letty prepared the table and poured the tea, Princess Maisy cleared her throat.

"When we're finished with tea, could you help me speak with

the seamstress and her assistant?" Princess Maisy asked.

"Of course," Letty replied. "Do you have more instructions for them?"

"Yes, sort of," said the princess. "Mostly, I want to apologize for how I behaved yesterday."

"I see," Letty said with a smile. "Yes, I would be happy to come with you."

When they were finished, Letty stacked the dishes back onto the kitchen cart as she always did. This time, though, Princess Maisy handed her dishes to Letty instead of making her come to collect them. "Just to make it easier," the princess explained with a faint blush.

A few minutes later, after walking back through the gardens and the hallways of the castle, Letty and Princess Maisy stood just outside the workshop that the seamstress and her assistant had been given.

"Are you sure it'll work?" Princess Maisy whispered, cautiously staring at the door of the workshop.

"I would guess so," Letty whispered back. "Most people appreciate an apology, but there's only one way to find out." She could hear the vague sounds of two voices muttering back and forth, so she knew they were working inside.

Princess Maisy closed her eyes and let out a deep breath, releasing the tension in her shoulders. She lifted her fist and knocked on the door.

Letty waited with anticipation for the door to open. She hoped she was right that this would go well. If it didn't, she worried that Princess Maisy would lose her resolve to keep their agreement.

Shuffling sounds came from inside the workshop, then the

scraping of a chair. After a moment, the door opened just enough for the seamstress's assistant to pop her head out. Her eyes widened at the sight of the princess.

"Your Highness!" she exclaimed. "Would you give me a moment, please?"

She shut the door before the princess could respond or hear the loud whispering from the room. Princess Maisy glanced at Letty nervously, and Letty gave a smile of encouragement. "You can do it," she whispered as softly as she could.

After a moment, the door opened again, this time wider, and the seamstress's face replaced the assistant.

"Lovely to see you, Your Highness," she said, although Letty thought her voice sounded strained. "How may we help you?"

"I just . . . I wanted to . . ." Princess Maisy stumbled over her words. She turned to Letty, looking helpless. Letty considered for a moment whether she should step in but decided against it. If the princess was really going to learn to be kind, she would have to practice. Letty waved her hand gently, gesturing for Princess Maisy to go on. The princess took another deep breath, turned back to the seamstress, and tried again.

"I just wanted to say I'm sorry," she said. Her words were shaky and came slowly, but they came nonetheless.

The seamstress's eyebrows rose, and her assistant's face suddenly appeared in the doorway again, behind the seamstress this time.

"The way I treated you yesterday was unacceptable," Princess Maisy continued, gaining confidence as she spoke. "I promise I will do better in the future, and I hope you will accept my apology."

Both the seamstress and her assistant stood still, mouths agape, for several long, uncomfortable seconds. At last, the seamstress shook her head, snapped her jaw closed, and responded, "Yes, yes, of course we do."

Princess Maisy breathed a sigh of relief. "Thank you," she said, a smile playing at the corners of her lips.

"It's our pleasure," the seamstress said. "Would you like to come in and discuss what we can do to suit the gowns more to your taste?"

"Yes, please."

The seamstress opened the door the rest of the way, providing space for the princess and Letty to enter. Before they stepped through the doorway, Princess Maisy looked over her shoulder at Letty. "I did it!" she mouthed enthusiastically. Letty beamed as she followed the princess into the workshop to discuss plans.

CHAPTER 3

P lease, take a seat, Your Highness," the seamstress said. Sewing
notions and piles of fabric covered nearly every surface in the
room. The seamstress's assistant apologetically cleared the assort-
ment of items from two stools and silently offered them to Letty
and Princess Maisy.

"Thank you," Princess Maisy said, gracefully taking her seat.
Letty sat down next to Princess Maisy, and the seamstress and her
assistant sat across from them, fidgeting nervously with their hands,
hair, and aprons.

"So, Your Highness, what can we do to fix those problems we
ran into yesterday?" the seamstress asked. She grabbed a notepad
from the cluttered table behind her and perched her pencil over
paper, ready to jot down each of the princess's requests.

Princess Maisy closed her eyes and breathed in deeply. "As I said,
I was unreasonable yesterday. The dresses you made are lovely, and I
think they will do perfectly for the prince's visit."

Letty looked at the princess in shock. "But, Your Highness, you
said—"

Princess Maisy waved her hand dismissively. "I know what I
said. If you don't mind, there are still some adjustments I would
like made to a few of the gowns, but there's no need to start from
scratch." She hesitated before adding the last of what she wanted to

say. "Except for the ball gown. The one you designed was beautiful, but it just doesn't suit me the way I would like," Princess Maisy explained.

The seamstress and her assistant exchanged relieved smiles. "Yes, of course, Your Highness. We can work on a sketch for that new gown today, and if you'd like, we can have you try on each gown again and let us know what changes you would like made."

With her assistant's help, the seamstress wheeled a rack of dresses over to Princess Maisy. "This one ripped yesterday as we were packing up," the assistant said, removing from the rack the delicate yellow dress the princess had tried on the day before. "But it only tore along one of the seams, so we should be able to fix it easily."

Letty helped the seamstress and her assistant slip Princess Maisy into each gown and fetched them pins to mark places that needed alterations—a pleat here, a little tuck there, a longer skirt on one dress, a different kind of sleeve on another. In less than an hour, all the alterations were pinned into the dresses and scribbled down on the seamstress's notepad, and a promising sketch for Princess Maisy's new ball gown had been drawn up. The atmosphere was light and happy, a stark contrast from the day before. All four women were smiling and seemed pleased with the progress being made.

"Thank you very much for your help," Princess Maisy said once they had finalized the last details.

"It's our pleasure," the seamstress beamed. She opened the door of the workshop for Letty and Princess Maisy.

The instant the door closed, Letty heard faintly from the other side, "Did that really just happen?" Letty grinned. She, too, could hardly believe how pleasant the visit had been.

"So, how did I do?" Princess Maisy asked, turning to Letty with a tentative smile.

"You did wonderfully. You were very kind and respectful. How do you feel it went?"

"It was good. I don't know how to explain it exactly, but it's nice to walk away from something like that without feeling frustrated with everyone around me."

"I'm glad," Letty replied.

Just then, clocks all throughout the castle simultaneously rang out four times to announce the hour.

"I'm late for my planning meeting," Princess Maisy said. "It's going to run long today, so don't worry about helping me get ready for supper—the cooks will serve supper during the meeting." Princess Maisy began walking away from Letty quickly, hurrying to get to her meeting. "And Letty," she said over her shoulder, "thank you for your help!"

"You're welcome," Letty replied, although she knew the princess likely couldn't hear her as she walked away. Once Princess Maisy had gone, Letty turned toward the stairs to work on preparing the guest bedrooms.

Often, other maids joined Letty in the afternoons to help her with the bedroom renovations she was making for the prince and his family, but today they were all occupied elsewhere in the castle. There was still much to do to prepare, and many of the projects were ones that Letty couldn't do alone. Letty did have one task she thought she could do by herself, though, which was to remove the old musty drapes from the windows and replace them with the new ones that had arrived earlier that afternoon from the best draper in Trielle.

Letty entered the first guest bedroom and immediately went to the thick paper parcel sitting next to the bed. She unwrapped it carefully until all the paper had been peeled away from the new drapes. They were even lovelier than she had imagined—tightly woven linen in a rich midnight-blue color adorned with elegant black floral accents. Letty admired the pattern, her fingertips gently tracing over it. *These will be much better*, she thought as she held them up to the old ones for comparison.

Letty stared up at the rod above the window. For a moment, she considered finding a footman to help her figure out how she was supposed to do this, but she quickly dismissed the idea. Everyone else was busy, and Letty felt uncomfortable asking someone to drop what they were doing to help her with such a simple task. "It won't be too hard, anyway," Letty murmured under her breath. She had never hung drapes before, but how difficult could it be?

Letty dragged the desk chair noisily across the room and planted it beneath the window. She piled the new drapes next to the chair and climbed up onto its seat, shifting her weight back and forth carefully to ensure she wouldn't fall. Satisfied that she was safe, Letty twisted the finial off the end of the rod and began to slide one old panel off. It took some effort to move the weighty material, but after a few moments, she managed to get the panel to the end of the rod and prepared to pull it off. But as Letty rustled the old heavy fabric, dust flew into the air, sending her into a sneezing fit. Her sneezes rocked her balance on the chair, and Letty felt herself beginning to tip over. Instinctively, she tried to steady herself by clutching on tighter to the drape, but instead of steadying her, Letty's tugging yanked the fabric off the rod. The cloth was heavier than she had expected. The weight pulled her even further off balance, and before Letty could process what was happening, she came crashing down, landing in a heap on top of the fallen drapes. A clatter came from somewhere in the room, but it didn't quite register with Letty; her attention was drawn to the throbbing she suddenly felt in her right shoulder. After a few stunned seconds, Letty finally collected her wits enough to check herself for any injuries. She grabbed her shoulder and felt around it gingerly. It was tender, and she suspected that it would bruise before long, but she didn't seem to be hurt any worse than that. Letty breathed a sigh of relief.

Down the hall, Letty heard the sounds of hurried footsteps. A moment later, the door swung open, and a young man appeared in the doorway. Letty recognized him as the footman who had gone to fetch the seamstress the day everyone first learned of the prince's upcoming visit. His name was Jacob, if Letty remembered correctly.

"Goodness!" he said, making eye contact with Letty, who was still lying on the floor. He rushed into the room and helped her to her feet. "What happened to you?" he asked.

"I was trying to hang the new drapes," Letty explained, her ears and face beginning to go bright pink. "But first, I had to take down the old ones, and I lost my balance, and then I sneezed . . ." she trailed off as she saw Jacob's amused smirk. Maybe she should have left out the part about sneezing.

"Sounds dangerous," he said. Jacob crossed in front of the window, then bent down to pick up the rod from the ground. It suddenly occurred to Letty that that was the clattering noise she had heard before—the rod and the other panel had dropped to the floor.

"And this fell before or after you did?" Jacob asked with no shift in his good-humored expression.

"I don't know," Letty murmured. She took the rod from him and tilted it to slide the second drape panel off, never making eye contact. "At the same time, I think."

Letty crouched down to fold the old drapes neatly, turning her back to Jacob and hoping that he would go away. She was mortified to have fallen doing something as simple as hanging drapes and even more so to have been found lying on the floor in a puddle of fabric. She put her hand on her aching shoulder again and rotated it a few times, trying to ease the pain.

"Aw, come on; I don't mean to tease. No hard feelings," Jacob said. He crouched down next to her and began helping her to fold the drapes. "Have you ever done this before?"

Letty shook her head but didn't give a verbal response. His implicit apology didn't erase her embarrassment.

"Well, normally, you would want to take down the rod with the drapes still on it. Sometimes it takes two people to do it, but it keeps the weight balanced so that it doesn't—well, you know." Jacob lifted the panel he was folding to emphasize his point.

"Thank you; I'll remember that for next time," Letty responded. No matter how embarrassed she was, she still wanted to be gracious. After all, it was kind of Jacob to help her.

"What about the other rooms? Have you taken the drapes down there?"

"No, not yet. I'll get to them once I put the new ones up in here." Letty glanced over at Jacob, the pink in her face finally subsiding as she began to feel more comfortable in the conversation. "And I'll make sure to do it correctly next time," she said with a grin.

"Why don't I go take care of those?" Jacob stood, already starting for the door. "It'll save you a little time."

"Oh, no, no," Letty quickly responded, "you don't have to do that. I can do it, I promise."

"I know you can, but it's no trouble. I was just bringing some things up to the library. If you slide the new drapes onto the rods, I'll come back through and hang them all up."

"No, really—" Letty started to say. She raised her hand, planning to wave Jacob away, but a jab of pain shot through her aching shoulder as she did. Letty winced and lowered her hand. Maybe she would be smart to avoid lifting those old heavy drapes, especially if it carried the possibility of taking another fall. "That would be very kind," Letty finally concluded. "Thank you."

Jacob nodded and slipped out of the room. Letty rolled her shoulder a few times slowly, hoping the aching would subside soon. After a moment, she stacked the old drapes into a tidy pile before sliding the new ones onto the rod. She quickly got comfortable with the motion, and when she no longer needed to look at her hands, she stared out the window. In the quiet, as she watched the clouds move through the sky, Letty wondered how the search party was faring. Were they still out there? Had they finally found her father? She could only imagine what was happening as they were out on the mountain. As she finished changing the drapes and doing her cleaning in the guest rooms, she prayed for a joyful reunion with her father.

CHAPTER 4

W hen Letty went to help Princess Maisy get ready for bed that night, she prepared to knock on the princess's door as she usually did. As she raised her hand, she winced at the pang she felt in her shoulder. *Left hand only for the next few days*, Letty reminded herself. She switched hands to rap on the door and opened it to see Princess Maisy lying on her bed, her hands pressed against her forehead.

"Are you all right, Your Highness?" Letty asked. She was a bit concerned to see the princess in that position—it was never a sign of a good mood.

"There's still so much to do," Princess Maisy groaned. "We can't get enough of the ingredients we need for meals, so I have to change entire meal plans. Invitations for the ball need to be sent out, but we haven't even figured out the guest list. Then there's the decorations, the musicians, the food for the ball . . . it's all so much." Princess Maisy's hands flopped out to the sides of her bed, and she heaved a deep sigh. "At least the guest bedrooms are nearly finished, aren't they?"

Letty shifted her weight from one leg to the other and began fidgeting with her hands. The princess was clearly stressed. Would she be upset with Letty if she knew how much work still needed to be done? Letty didn't think so. After all, the princess had promised that she would try not to get overly upset about the details, and she had done well so far. Why should any of that change now?

"The rooms will be finished before the prince and his family arrive," Letty said, "but there's still quite a bit of work to be done. The new drapes were hung today, and the maids and I have finished polishing, dusting, and deep cleaning everything."

Princess Maisy propped herself up on her elbows. An accusatory tone crept into her voice, accompanied by an elegantly arched eyebrow. "What else needs to be done?" she asked.

Letty hesitated. She didn't want to add to the princess's worries, but she couldn't simply ignore her question. "Most of the furniture still needs to be varnished. The desk and chair are finished in one bedroom, but everything else still needs a new coat of varnish," Letty explained.

"And how long will that take?"

"Well, I'm not exactly sure," said Letty. "But—"

"What do you mean you're not sure?" Princess Maisy sat up taller, and the pitch of her voice rose as she did. "Haven't you asked anyone or done any research? Have you planned at all? How can you be positive that it will be done before the prince arrives?"

"It takes some time to dry, but I—I just assumed . . ." Letty trailed off.

The princess's eyes were wide, almost frantic with distress. She closed them for a moment and took a deep breath. "Fine," Princess Maisy said at last. "If that's all that's left, I trust that you can finish it in time. We'll have to make sure other maids will be available to help you." Princess Maisy forced a smile. "At least everything we need has been ordered at this point, right?"

Letty didn't respond. Almost everything had been ordered, but

Letty had been so caught up in all the other elements of the guest bedrooms that she had completely forgotten her plan to add artwork to the walls. Furthermore, Letty had been busy trying to make sure everything was right with the princess's gowns. It seemed there couldn't be a worse time to explain this to Princess Maisy.

Letty's body language gave away her answer. When Letty looked down, the princess sat up even straighter and drew a deep, tense breath. "I asked so little of you," she said through clenched teeth. "It's not as though I wanted you to plan the whole visit. All I requested is that you get the guest bedrooms in order so the prince and his parents can have somewhere comfortable to stay, and yet here we are, a week away from the visit, and you aren't even close to finished! Are you lazy or simply incompetent? Or perhaps this is some silly test you've set up to see if I'll do things 'your way' as I promised, but that promise did not mean that I was going to dismiss my standards. There's only so much I can do on my own, Letty. If you will not do the simple tasks I give you, how am I going to finish any of the preparations on time?" The princess pressed her hands against her forehead again and flopped back onto the bed. "I need a peppermint bath, please. Immediately."

"Yes, Your Highness," Letty mumbled. As Letty shuffled about, preparing the princess's bath, she wondered if Princess Maisy regretted her choice in asking Letty to stay. After all, it had only been twenty-four hours, and already the princess was back to being upset with her. And why shouldn't she be? Letty had made a mistake, this one fairly large. She wondered if she had made the wrong choice to stay and serve the princess. The princess had reverted back to insults the moment things went wrong. Was it impossible to have a mature conversation about Princess Maisy's concerns without being peppered with accusations and insults?

As her nostrils filled with the sweet, crisp scent of peppermint oil, Letty prayed that she wasn't too late to find artwork for the bedrooms before the prince and his family arrived. She also prayed for the patience to get through this night and work things out with Princess Maisy.

"Your Highness," Letty said softly as she walked back to the princess's room, "your bath is ready for you."

Princess Maisy merely grunted in reply. After a few moments of silence, the princess peeled herself away from her bed and moped into the bathroom.

Letty sat thinking on a small stool next to the armoire as she waited for the princess to finish her bath. Once again, she found herself unsure how to approach an apology when neither she nor the princess were entirely in the wrong. On one hand, Princess Maisy was right that Letty should have had a clearer plan to be sure everything, including ordering the artwork, was done on time. On the other hand, Princess Maisy had no idea how physically taxing some of the tasks were. Even though Jacob had taken down the curtain rods for her, Letty's aching shoulder had made it impossible to get the new drapes up very quickly, and she knew that scraping and sanding down all of the furniture would take ages if it were only up to her and a few maids. But how could she explain this without turning it into an argument? After a bit of consideration, Letty determined that she would write a note.

Letty took a scrap of paper and a pencil from the bottom drawer of Princess Maisy's vanity. She thought carefully about how to phrase her note, unconsciously rotating her sore shoulder as she did so.

Your Highness, Letty began writing at last.

I'm very sorry to have upset you. You're right; it's too close to the prince's arrival to still be unsure about when the guest bedrooms will be finished. Unfortunately, with the rest of the maids so busy, they have not been able to help me often, and I've found it very difficult to do some of these things on my own. Hanging new drapes, for example, led to me hurting my shoulder, which made the task take longer than it should have. I hope you understand that I really am doing my best. As I get more help, things should go more quickly.

Sincerely, Letty.

She reread the note quickly to make sure that she hadn't forgotten anything she wanted to say. Then, satisfied, Letty carefully folded the note and placed it next to Princess Maisy's pillow. She wasn't sure if she and the princess would discuss the problem that night, but even if they didn't, at least Princess Maisy could read the note when she was ready.

Princess Maisy dragged her feet as she came back into her bedroom, her hair dripping onto the shoulders of the nightgown Letty had laid out for her. Without speaking, she plopped down into the vanity chair. Letty stood behind Princess Maisy and hesitantly began brushing through her wet hair.

"Are you feeling all right, Your Highness?" Letty asked gently. The princess's face was drawn into a somber frown, and the bags under her eyes seemed deeper than before. She sat hunched over in her chair rather than sitting up straight as she normally did.

"Not really," Princess Maisy muttered. "I'm tired. I think I'll go to bed once we're done."

"Of course. I'll be done soon," Letty promised. She quickly finished brushing and used a towel to squeeze the extra water out of

Princess Maisy's hair. "All right, I'm finished. Is there anything else you'd like from me before you go to bed?" Usually there were several other steps in Princess Maisy's nightly routine.

"No, you can go. I just want to sleep," Princess Maisy said. She crossed the room and climbed into her bed. She didn't seem to notice the note Letty had placed on her bed, but Letty figured that it might be better for Princess Maisy to read it in the morning when she wasn't so tired anyway.

"Good night, Your Highness," Letty whispered as she shut the door. When it was securely closed, Letty leaned against the princess's door and sighed heavily. It had been a long day, and the evening had felt even longer. She didn't blame the princess for wanting to go to bed early. As a matter of fact, Letty was looking forward to crawling into bed herself.

"Letty," a loud whisper came suddenly from her right. Letty spun around to see her friend Elias, the young stable boy, standing at the end of the hall. "Oh good, I hoped you would be finished helping the princess," he said. "Your brother Miles is here. He wants to see you."

CHAPTER 5

L etty's heart thudded as she followed Elias down the grand
staircase. Elias had not mentioned anyone being with Miles.
Surely Papa would have come if the search party had found him,
wouldn't he? Then again, if Papa were ill or hurt, he wouldn't be
able to come to the castle right away; he would still be at home
resting. Her stomach twisted in knots. Letty wished she at least
knew what to expect.

Elias separated from Letty once they reached the bottom of the
stairs. "He's outside," Elias explained. "See you later."

Elias was so nonchalant and carefree about the whole thing.
Letty knew she shouldn't read into it; he probably didn't have any
idea what was going on. But she couldn't help but feel that maybe
his reaction meant the news would be good.

And then there was Miles, standing near the doorway, leaning
against his crutches more heavily than usual. His energy seemed to
have been drained from him. All the hope that Letty had been
feeling, the anticipation building up inside her, vanished the instant
she saw Miles's face in the light from the great hall. His eyebrows
were knit together, and the corners of his mouth drooped. His eyes
looked dull and defeated.

"Miles?" Letty's voice shook.

"Hi, Letty," Miles said with a smile that didn't reach his eyes.

"Mind if we take a walk?" He tilted his head toward the gardens.

Letty simply nodded in response. Any words that she wanted to say were caught in her throat.

They walked together in near silence for a few minutes, the only noise coming from Miles's crutches as they knocked into rocks or crossed over stone pathways. Letty desperately wanted to stay quiet and avoid the conversation that would inevitably bring so much heartbreak, but the words needed to be said.

"They didn't find Papa," Letty said at last. It wasn't a question; she already knew the answer.

"No," Miles answered softly, "they didn't. The search party tried so hard, Letty, but it seems he just wasn't there."

A single tear slid down Letty's face. "So where is he?" she pleaded. She knew, of course, that Miles didn't have an answer, but she needed him to say *something*.

Miles didn't speak for a moment. At last, he replied, "At this point, I think we have to assume that Papa is—" His voice broke. Hearing her big brother get emotional made Letty's heart ache even more. "I think we have to assume that he's gone."

How could Miles say such a thing? He was ever the optimist. If he had truly given up hope, that meant there was simply none left.

"What about the shop?" Letty asked after a few more moments of silence, desperate to focus on something less laden with finality.

"What about it?"

"Are you going to keep it open?"

Miles shrugged. "I don't really know. I don't plan to open up for a few days. After that, I suppose I'll get back to it. I don't know what else I would do."

"Miles, is that you?" a voice came from somewhere nearby.

"Yes, I'm here," Miles called back. "It's Peter," he explained, turning to Letty. "I needed his help getting here and back again."

"What about Mama?" Letty asked. "Why didn't she come with you?"

Miles hesitated. "Mama didn't seem ready to come here tonight. She's not taking the news well."

Letty's heart dropped even further. "Poor Mama. Is she all right?"

"She will be," Miles assured her. "She just needs to rest for a little while, I think."

By that point, Peter had joined them. "Hey, Letty," he said. He wrapped his arms around her, pulling her into a tight hug. "I'm so sorry. We tried so hard to find him—"

"I know," Letty interrupted. "Thank you."

"Do you need to leave, Peter?" Miles asked.

"I don't want to pull you away, but I do need to get home soon," Peter replied apologetically.

"That's all right," Miles said. "We can go. Are you going to be OK, Letty?"

Letty didn't know what to say. Of course she wasn't OK. Her papa had been missing for weeks, and now she was supposed to accept the conclusion that he was no longer alive? She desperately wanted to be with Miles and grieve, but she knew he needed to get home to Mama. Frankly, even if she had the strength to go back home that night, she doubted she would manage to get back to the castle in the morning.

"I'll be fine," she finally told him.

"All right. Please come home when you can, any time you would like." He wrapped his arms around Letty as tightly as he could with his crutches in the way. The pressure from his hug pushed against her sore shoulder, causing it to start aching again. "I love you, Letty," Miles said as he pulled away.

"I love you too." Letty barely managed to get the words out.

She remained rooted to the spot as she watched Miles lean against Peter for support and start back down the path toward Lantern Lane. As they disappeared into the darkness, Letty felt more alone than she could ever remember, even in her first days at the castle. For a moment, she considered calling after them and begging Miles to stay, but she knew she couldn't. Miles needed to get home to be with Mama, and Peter was likely exhausted from searching all day. Letty could no longer control the flood of tears that had been building. She turned and bolted farther into the gardens. She didn't care where she was going or how cold the air was that whipped around her; she simply ran until her lungs could no longer stand the strain of her movement combined with her tears. She dropped to the ground. The spot where she fell was very familiar to her: right next to her face was the hardy winter rosebush she plucked a bloom from each day on the way to tea. The flowers reminded her so much of home. The reminder wasn't as comforting now, though. She knew that her father wasn't at home and likely never would be again. The thought consumed her, and wrenching sobs overtook Letty's body.

"Papa," she sobbed. "I miss you so much. You can't be gone. What am I supposed to do?" The lump in her throat became so large that she couldn't speak anymore, but it didn't matter: saying it out loud was no better than simply thinking it. Neither would change anything.

"You'll be OK, Letty," a soft, deep voice spoke from the

darkness. Letty sat up suddenly, so startled that she stopped crying. "I love you," the voice came again. Letty recognized that voice with its soothing tone and tender strength.

"Papa?" She could not tell where his voice had come from. Her head whipped around, and she peered through the darkness for any sign of him. She hastily wiped her eyes with the backs of her hands to help clear her vision. "Papa!" she cried again. No voice answered her. No footsteps came toward her. No figure appeared from around the corners of the castle walls or from the expansive gardens. Had she only imagined it? Was she so desperate for her father that she was hallucinating? Letty stood and padded a bit farther into the gardens. "Please, Papa," she said weakly, tears refilling her eyes. "If you're there somewhere, please come to me."

For a moment, she waited in silence with bated breath, heart thudding in her chest. Slowly, she counted down from ten, insisting to herself that if Papa didn't come to her or speak again when she got to zero, she would chalk it up to her imagination.

"Ten, nine, eight," she whispered slowly, her eyes fluttering back and forth over everything around her. "Seven, six, five, four . . ." She turned in a full circle a few times, ensuring she wouldn't miss a thing nearby. "Three, two—" Letty caught her breath. There, coming from around the corner of the castle . . .

With the distance and the darkness, it was difficult to make out the details, but there was someone there, she was sure of it. Letty paced a few steps toward the figure. The thudding in her chest got faster and harder. Yes, someone was there walking toward her. Could it be?

"One," Letty breathed, ready to rush forward. At that moment, the figure raised a lamp with a dim candle flickering inside. Though the light was faint, it illuminated just enough to shatter Letty's heart to pieces.

"Letty?" the figure said, walking more quickly toward her now. It wasn't her papa's voice. This voice was high and lilting, not strong and deep. Letty never would have thought she would be so disappointed to hear Jocelyn say her name.

"Thank goodness, there you are!" Jocelyn said, running up to Letty and wrapping her arms around her. "Elias told me that Miles was here, and I figured he must be bringing you news. But then I saw through the window that he and his friend were leaving, and I didn't hear you come back in, and I was so worried—but you've been crying," she noticed at last as she pulled away. "The news wasn't good, was it?"

"No," Letty replied, trying quickly to dry her eyes. She had cried in front of Jocelyn before, but she felt she couldn't now. If she wasn't with Miles or Mama, she wanted to mourn her father alone.

"Oh, Letty, I'm sorry," Jocelyn said. She pulled Letty into a hug again. "Come, let's go inside where it's warm—you're shivering."

It was freezing out, that was true, but Letty's trembling was due more to her grief and stress than the weather. Still, she let herself be led back into the castle. As they walked, Letty wondered whether she should tell Jocelyn about hearing her father's voice. The longer she considered it, the more she talked herself out of it. It was embarrassing to admit she'd imagined such a thing—surely it *was* her imagination. Besides, she was so tired, and explaining it would be too exhausting. She decided to give herself time to process it all before she told anyone about it.

Jocelyn helped Letty up to her room, gave her a glass of water, and set a nightgown at the foot of Letty's bed.

CHAPTER 5

"Is there anything else you need?" Jocelyn asked softly.

Letty shook her head as she lay on her bed. There *were* other things she needed, but she didn't know how to express them. She didn't even know exactly what they were.

"Sleep well then, Letty. And again, I'm so sorry."

The moment the door closed, Letty released a deep breath and, with it, let go of all the emotions she had been trying to hold in. The tears flowed freely once again, interrupted by hiccups. She tried to remain as silent as she could so as not to disturb the princess down the hall. She remained curled up on her bed, knees hugged to her chest, whimpering through the flood of tears for hours until she physically couldn't cry anymore. After she was finished, she lay for some time, lingering with the aching she was beginning to feel in her chest and the throbbing that continued in her shoulder. At long last, she drifted off into a restless sleep, but before she did, the words she thought she had heard earlier repeated in her mind once again, *You'll be OK, Letty. I love you.*

CHAPTER 6

Letty stared at the ceiling as she listened to her clock chime to wake her—not that she needed to be woken. She had tossed and turned all night and had been lying awake for the past twenty minutes.

I have to get up, Letty thought, but her body disagreed. *I have to wake Princess Maisy. There are things we need to do today*, Letty tried to convince herself as her limbs seemed to sink further into the mattress, and her heavy eyelids begged her to try to go back to sleep. Letty desperately wished she could give in, but she remembered how frustrated and distressed Princess Maisy had been the night before. She couldn't contribute to another day like that. As little of herself as Letty felt she had to give, if she couldn't do her best that day, the princess deserved to know why.

Letty managed to pry herself out of bed and stretch her limbs, tense from being curled so uncomfortably all night. Her shoulder stung as she moved it, but Letty ignored that. Since she hadn't changed into her nightgown the night before—it had seemed too difficult—she needed a fresh dress. She trudged over to her wardrobe and removed the first dress her hand touched without bothering to look at it. She tugged it over her head, replacing the one she had worn last night, which she now saw was stained at the knees by grass and dirt and was still damp at the collar from her tears. Then she pulled her hair into a loose, messy ponytail at the nape of her neck. It would be good enough for today.

Letty glanced at herself in the mirror. Her eyes were puffy and purple bags were forming underneath. Her face was still blotchy and red, and, as she had noticed of Miles last night, it looked like all of the energy had been drained out of her. Quite frankly, she looked completely unpresentable, but it was only minutes from seven o'clock, and she had a hard time bringing herself to care enough to put any more effort into her appearance.

Letty trudged down the hall toward the princess's room to begin the day as usual. She felt as if a dark cloud followed her through the corridors of the castle, but she tried to ignore it.

"Good morning, Your Highness," Letty mumbled, trying but failing to act like her usual chipper self. She opened Princess Maisy's armoire and began rustling through the gowns. "What would you like to wear today?"

The bed creaked behind her as Princess Maisy sat up.

"I'm not sure," she yawned. "Something green, maybe."

Letty ran her fingers along the hanging fabrics until she found one with a simple cut in a stunning shade of emerald. "Is this acceptable?" she asked, turning to hold the dress up for the princess to see.

"Yes," Princess Maisy said after a quick appraisal. She drew back slightly when she saw Letty's face. "What happened to you? You look miserable."

Letty had planned to tell Princess Maisy what had happened right away, but as she looked at the princess now, Letty faltered. What was she supposed to say? That her father was gone, and at this point it seemed clear that he wasn't coming back? She knew that as soon as she said anything of the sort, she wouldn't be able to keep herself from crying again, and she desperately did not want to cry in front of the princess.

Letty's eyes flitted around the room for a moment before she responded, "I just didn't sleep very well last night." She forced herself to swallow the lump that rose in her throat. She would not cry in front of the princess!

Princess Maisy looked skeptical as she examined Letty a bit closer. "If you say so," she relented.

Princess Maisy climbed out of bed and took the dress from Letty. She seemed much calmer than the night before.

"You're looking better," Letty said, changing the topic as the princess disappeared behind her dressing curtain.

"I feel much better," Princess Maisy replied. "I think I just needed a good night's sleep to clear my head." She paused for a moment. "And a kind note didn't hurt, either. Thank you for leaving it, Letty. I understand that you are trying, and I overreacted last night. Again." She stepped out from behind her dressing curtain, and Letty went to lace up the back of her dress. "I know I said it before, but I really will try to calm down. Everything will work out. I just need to stop worrying so much about it, I'm sure."

Letty finished lacing the dress, doing her best not to move her right arm too much, and knelt down to make sure the hem was adjusted properly. Princess Maisy looked down at her. "Are you sure you're all right, Letty?" she asked.

Letty knew she should just tell Princess Maisy about Papa and what had happened the night before. There was no reason not to, and she knew that, but she couldn't bring herself to do it. She forced a pained smile. "I'm fine. Quickly, let's get your hair done. I wouldn't want you to be late for breakfast."

The morning routine was unusually silent that day. It was strange for Letty to avoid making small talk as she brushed Princess Maisy's hair and finished getting her ready for the day—typically, if anyone avoided talking, it was the princess, but today, Letty found it difficult to carry on a conversation.

"I've got to finalize the guest list for the ball today," Princess Maisy offered after a few minutes of uncomfortable silence. "We'll have to pore over lists of all the nobles in the kingdom and figure out who we can invite."

"That sounds difficult," Letty muttered, not looking away from the small braid she was weaving in the princess's hair.

"It shouldn't be terribly hard," Princess Maisy responded. "We don't have many noblemen in Trielle, but my uncle said it is very important to make sure the highest ranking of them attend the ball. The harder part may be deciding whether we want to fill the ballroom by inviting others as well." The princess chuckled as she spoke the last sentence.

Letty only smiled vaguely in return. She heard what Princess Maisy was saying, but she wasn't really listening. She was imagining herself kneeling by the winter rosebush last night. And that voice— it wouldn't stop replaying in her head. It had been so distinct, so clear, not like her imagination at all. But it had to be her imagination, didn't it? If it had really been Papa speaking to her, he would have come to her or responded when she called, not disappeared again as she became more frantic. Yes, it had to be her imagination. But what if . . .

"Letty?" Princess Maisy finally interrupted Letty's train of thought. "What are you doing?"

Letty looked down at her hands, which were now mindlessly twisting the end of the princess's braid around her finger. She hadn't realized just how lost she had been in her own head.

"Just making sure it's got a good curl on the end," Letty said quickly, though not quite convincingly. "I think it's good enough now."

"Oh, all right," Princess Maisy responded with clear skepticism in her voice.

Letty passed Princess Maisy a towel after she washed her face. She found the princess's beeswax for her lips, which Princess Maisy worried were becoming dry, and helped the princess tie her shoes. Throughout all of these tasks, silence permeated the room. Princess Maisy kept glancing over at Letty out of the corners of her eyes. Letty knew she was behaving strangely, but she was too tired and distracted to do much more than what was required this morning.

At last, the princess's morning routine was complete, and it was time to go downstairs for breakfast. Letty accompanied the princess down, surprised at how much concentration it took for her to walk down the grand stone steps with her head as foggy as it was.

"I'll be waiting in the library after breakfast," Letty said, although she really didn't need to. It was no different from their normal routine.

Princess Maisy smiled regardless. "Enjoy your breakfast," she said as she entered the dining hall.

Letty dragged her feet down the long hallway behind the stairs. It felt longer than usual, just as the door felt heavier than it normally did when she pulled it open. The kitchen was in its usual hubbub. Letty's nose filled with the sweet smells of cinnamon, baked apples, and blueberries. Cooks and kitchen hands bustled about, stirring bubbling pots and chopping fresh vegetables to be used later in the day, and a small group of maids, guards, and footmen sat around one of the tables, chatting loudly. A few other servants stood in line to get their food—muffins, it looked like. At the front of the line, Letty spotted Jocelyn's swinging strawberry-blonde braid, the only part of her that was visible around the much taller servants between them.

Jocelyn looked over her shoulder. She was carrying a serving tray with two muffins and some fruit. She started walking toward the door of the kitchen but stopped when she saw Letty standing in the doorway. Her eyebrows lifted, and she increased her pace as she walked toward Letty.

"What are you doing down here?" Jocelyn asked.

Letty cocked her head to the side. "What do you mean? Where else would I be?"

"In bed! You shouldn't be up working after last night; you should be resting or going home to your family."

"I'm fine—" Letty started to say, but Jocelyn wouldn't have it.

"You are not fine. You didn't sleep at all last night, did you?" Jocelyn pushed the tray she had been carrying into Letty's hands and put one arm around Letty's waist to turn her around.

"Not very much," Letty admitted.

"I can't believe the princess made you work in this condition. One would think she'd at least be sympathetic to your loss."

"I didn't tell her yet. Princess Maisy hasn't done anything wrong. She doesn't know."

Jocelyn stopped. "Letty, why in the world wouldn't you tell her?"

Hot tears pooled in Letty's eyes. She blinked quickly, trying to get rid of them before they could fall. "I don't know. I just couldn't say it." Why was she so close to crying? Letty didn't expect herself not to be upset, but surely she could hold in her emotions for a few hours at a time.

"Oh, Letty." Jocelyn hugged her as well as she could without knocking the tray of food out of Letty's hands. "Let's get you back to bed. You can sleep for a little while longer and then go home."

"But Princess Maisy has so much that needs to be done today, and the guest bedrooms aren't nearly ready—"

"I'll take care of the princess," Jocelyn insisted, "and the guest bedrooms. There are plenty of us to do that. There's only one Letty to go be with her mother and brother. I promise it will not be the end of the world if you don't work today. Do you understand?"

Letty nodded slowly. Jocelyn was right, of course.

"Good. So you're going to go upstairs, eat your breakfast, take a nap, and go home, right?" Jocelyn confirmed.

"Right."

Jocelyn smiled, but it was the same kind of smile that Miles had given the night before or that Letty had offered the princess that morning—a lips-closed smile, one that didn't quite reach the eyes. Letty's heart broke and swelled at the same time. There was no reason that Jocelyn had to be upset on Letty's behalf, but Letty was so grateful that she was.

"Thank you, Jocelyn."

"Of course. Now, off to bed with you, go."

CHAPTER 7

The sun beamed into Letty's bedroom through her periwinkle curtains. She rolled over in bed and rubbed the sleep from her eyes with a yawn. *What time is it?* Letty wondered, casting her eyes around to find the clock hanging on her wall. It was almost lunchtime. She considered closing her eyes again—another few hours of rest certainly wouldn't hurt, but she already felt much better than she had that morning, at least in terms of fatigue. Letty pulled her legs over the side of the bed and jammed her feet into the boots she had barely managed to kick off before falling asleep. The muffins Jocelyn had sent upstairs with Letty still sat on her tiny nightstand, and Letty's stomach grumbled at the sight of them. Sleep had won out over hunger, and her stomach was protesting now. Her fingers hovered indecisively over the two flavors on the tray before she picked up a muffin and sank her teeth in. It was a bit dry and not quite as good as the ones Peter always gave her from his family's bakery, but still, it was satisfying.

She sat for a moment munching on a late breakfast, wishing everything around her weren't so silent. It was difficult not to miss Papa when there was nothing to distract her from thoughts of him. *I should really go home, like Jocelyn said,* she thought, *but I can't leave the castle without letting Princess Maisy know and making sure it's all right.* She would have to find Princess Maisy.

Letty pulled her shawl off the back of a chair and draped it over one arm so that she was ready to go if the princess approved. Princess Maisy should just be finishing up her lessons, so Letty assumed she would be able to find her in the library.

Letty pulled the library door open as slowly and quietly as she could to see inside without interrupting the lessons. She put her eye up to the crack and peered in. She couldn't see Princess Maisy, but that should have been obvious. The table the princess always took her lessons at was in the corner of the room, which she would never be able to see from her position. She did hear pages rustling, though. She decided to risk poking her head in just a bit farther.

The door creaked as she tugged on it. Letty winced, hoping she hadn't disturbed anything.

"Your Highness?" came the tutor's voice from inside.

Letty slipped the rest of the way into the room, standing just inside the doorway where the tutor, who was alone in the library, could see her. "No, just me, Letty. The princess's lady-in-waiting," she explained.

The tutor cocked one of his bushy white eyebrows. "Ah, I see. What can I do for you, miss?" he asked.

"Are the princess's lessons over already?"

"Yes, we finished a few minutes early today." He straightened the pile of books he had stacked on the table. "I have to say, I was surprised you were not here for Princess Maisy's lessons. I assumed you must be sick." Although he was not directly asking for an explanation, the way he glanced at her over the rims of his glasses made it clear that he was at least a bit curious.

"Jocelyn—that is, one of the maids—insisted that I sleep in a bit," Letty replied, not particularly inclined to share the more personal details with a near stranger.

"The short one with the reddish hair?" the tutor asked.

Letty smiled. "Yes, that's Jocelyn."

He nodded approvingly. "Ah, I know her. She's a good one. She was here just a minute ago. You could probably still catch up if you're trying to find her."

"I was looking for Princess Maisy, actually, but I'll just wait until she's finished with luncheon."

"All right, well, good afternoon to you, miss."

Letty dropped into a quick, shallow curtsy. "Good afternoon." She ducked out of the library and started toward the stairs, figuring she might as well go down to the kitchen while she waited for the princess.

"Letty!"

Letty turned her head to see Jocelyn coming down the hall from the direction of her bedroom.

"I was just coming to check if you needed anything," Jocelyn explained, gesturing back toward the hall.

"Thank you, Jocelyn. I think I'm all right. I'm just waiting for Princess Maisy to finish with luncheon to make sure I can go home."

"Oh, don't worry about that. I told the princess what happened and that you would be going home today. She understands."

"Really?" Letty scrunched her eyebrows together. "Are you sure it won't be a problem if I leave now?"

Jocelyn put her hand on Letty's arm. "Yes, Letty, I'm positive. You need to stop worrying. Just go home, rest, and spend some time with your family."

Letty opened her mouth again, about to ask when she should be back, but Jocelyn stopped her before she could speak.

"You can come back when you're ready," she interjected. "Don't worry too much about the details. The princess knows you'll be gone, and she understands, so go home."

Letty breathed a sigh of relief. "If you say so." She pulled the soft violet shawl on her arm around her shoulders. "I'll see you soon, then. Thank you for your help."

"Of course. And give my condolences to your mother and Miles," she said as they walked down the steps.

Letty waved goodbye as she went through the castle doors into the bright, brisk early afternoon. She blinked against the crisp breeze blowing directly into her face. The snow was thick on the mountains, and the heavy clouds in the sky looked eager to send more. Letty strode home, her long legs stretching over the cobblestones, carrying her quickly down Lantern Lane. She passed the mapmaker's shop, the blacksmith's shop, and Peter's family's bakery. As she passed the bakery, Letty began to slow. A knot formed in her stomach. Suddenly, she wondered if she was ready to go back to a home she knew her father would never return to. Even when she had been hopeful about his return, home had felt different. Would it even be bearable now? And what about Mama? Miles had said the night before that Mama wasn't doing very well. Letty could only imagine walking into the closed-down shop and seeing the dust accumulating on the shelves, walking up the stairs at the back into a dark, cold, quiet home. She envisioned Mama lying in bed, too heartbroken to bake or even get up, while Miles, doing all he could to take care of her, was sitting alone at the kitchen table. The thought was almost too much to bear.

Letty continued, slowly now, down Lantern Lane. Before long, she came upon the cobbler's shop. She hesitated in the front.

Maybe it wouldn't hurt to stop in to see her favorite little friends for a moment first. It would give her a much-needed boost before facing reality at home.

Letty strolled around to the back of the building. The same gingham curtains hung in the window, but no children waited for her there. She could hear one of the twin infants wailing.

Letty pulled her lips into a smile and tapped on the door. A few seconds later, she heard shuffling coming from inside before the door swung open.

Letty had come expecting to be cheered up, but instantly, it became clear that maybe it was Letty who needed to do the cheering. Liam and Elsie's mother, Kiana, stood in the doorway holding her crying baby on one hip and using the back of her other hand to wipe at her red eyes. Her eyes widened as she looked into Letty's face.

"Letty! What a wonderful surprise!" Kiana's face broke into a strained smile. "Please, come in."

"Is everything all right?" Letty asked, accepting the invitation to come inside.

Kiana avoided the question. "Liam and Elsie are just supposed to be waking up from their nap. I'll go get them." Kiana picked up a handkerchief lying on the kitchen table and used it to wipe her eyes and face better than her hand could. She bounced her baby on her hip, making shushing sounds to try to calm him.

"I can hold the baby if you would like," Letty offered. Although Kiana hadn't answered her question, Letty guessed that the baby's fussing might be the reason she was upset.

"Thank you very much," said Kiana. Letty happily took the infant in her arms, careful to support most of his weight with her uninjured arm, and began swaying and cooing. "I'll be right back," Kiana added before padding back to the short hallway off to the side of the kitchen.

Within just a few moments, the baby's wailing turned to a whimper, and his tiny eyes fluttered closed. He snuggled into Letty's chest, and she paced gently back and forth in front of the kitchen table, bouncing him lightly.

"Letty! Letty! Letty!" two voices chirped in chorus from the back room. The excited clip-clopping of skipping feet echoed until Liam and Elsie appeared in the kitchen. Liam beamed, and Elsie squealed loudly. They both dashed as fast as their legs could carry them across the small kitchen over to Letty.

"Hello, friends!" Letty said in a loud whisper. The baby squirmed in her arms at the noise. "Let's be quiet for just a second—baby brother is sleeping." Kiana followed her toddlers back out into the kitchen, chuckling at her children's excitement.

"I can't believe you got him asleep already," Kiana said. She lifted the infant from Letty's arms. "I've been trying for an hour. Hopefully, his brother won't wake him up too soon. I'll just go lay him down quickly."

With the baby out of her arms, Letty was able to kneel down to get on Liam and Elsie's level. "It's been so long since I've seen you," Letty said, opening her arms for the children to run into. "You've both gotten so big!" Elsie giggled, and Liam puffed up his little chest with pride.

"I'm the tallest!" said Liam.

"You are very tall," Letty acknowledged with a grin. "So, what new adventures have you two had since the last time I saw you?" she asked.

"The men have to go look for Pappy," Elsie said.

That was not at all the answer she had expected. Letty's smile fell as she tried to process what Elsie had said. Was it possible that she had misheard or that the little girl had misspoken?

"What was that?" Letty asked.

"Pappy isn't home," Liam said somberly. "Mammy said the men have to go look for him."

Letty's head spun wildly. Was this some new game they were playing? Had Kiana told the children about her father, and now they were using it for make-believe?

Kiana stepped slowly out of the back rooms and into the kitchen. Letty looked up at her face from her perch on the ground with the children. Kiana's lips were pursed, and the tears she had been wiping away when Letty arrived were returning now.

"What do they mean?" Letty asked her.

"Rylan went out the other night to run a few errands," Kiana explained in a strained voice. "I waited up for him, but he didn't come home. Of course, I was worried, but I assumed he would be back the next morning with some kind of explanation. But he wasn't." Kiana's lips pursed together tighter as though they were the only barrier against her tears.

"How long has he been gone?" Letty asked softly.

"Two nights so far. I wondered at first if maybe he had just waited somewhere to join the search party for your father when they went out, but then they came home yesterday, and no one had seen him."

Letty held Liam and Elsie a bit tighter in her arms. "I'm so sorry," she said. "I'm sure they'll find him soon."

"I hope so." Kiana's voice cracked. "I don't know yet how big the search party will be. Everyone wants to help, of course, but there's only so much time they can take away from their businesses."

Letty nodded her head. What a terrible situation. Two men missing from Lantern Lane so close together? It was so tragic and so wildly confusing. What was happening?

"I'm sure it will be fine." Although Letty tried to make her voice reassuring, both she and Kiana knew that the words were mostly empty. It was a wish, not a promise.

Liam tapped Letty's arm to get her attention. "I want to look for Pappy too," he said. "I can help. I'm big."

Letty laughed and ruffled the little boy's hair. "I'm sure you would be a great help, Liam," she assured him, "but right now, I think you can be the biggest help at home taking care of your Mammy. Do you think you can do that?"

Liam nodded, once again puffing out his little chest to show Letty how big and strong he was.

"Me too?" Elsie asked.

"Yes, you too. You can help take care of your baby brothers."

Elsie grinned. "I like that." She stared into Letty's eyes for a moment before asking, "Did you bring us candy?"

"Elsie," Kiana scolded, but Letty only laughed. It was refreshing to spend time with someone so innocent that sweets could be a distraction from any trouble.

"Not this time, I'm sorry. I'll bring you candy soon, though. I promise." She extended her pinky finger out to Elsie, and Elsie interlocked it with her own, securing the promise. Liam waved his finger in front of Letty to get a pinky promise of his own. When the pinky promises had been officially made, Letty stood. "I should probably be getting home," she said, "but is there anything I can do for you before I leave?"

Kiana shook her head no. "You've been so much help just by coming to visit. Thank you for stopping by, Letty."

Kiana walked her to the door and opened it but put one hand gently on Letty's shoulder before she could leave. Kiana leaned in closer to Letty so she could speak softly enough that her children would not hear. "I'm so sorry about your father," she said in a strained, crackling whisper. "The search party did everything they could. I will be praying for you and your family."

"And I will be praying for yours," Letty responded, fighting back the tears that threatened to rise in her own eyes.

"Bye, Letty!" Liam and Elsie cried as the door closed behind her.

Letty's heart broke for the little ones as she walked away from their home and toward her own. She said a brief, silent prayer that their father's tale would not end as Papa's had.

CHAPTER 8

Letty opened the unlocked door of her father's shop and was immediately greeted by a strange smell wafting down the stairs. Was something burning? As quickly as she could, Letty crossed the dimly lit room, ignoring the shelves and windowsills that were beginning to show clear signs of going undusted for the last few days.

"What's that smell?" Letty shouted up the stairs as she made her way up.

"Letty!" came Miles's voice from the kitchen. "Thank goodness you're here."

Letty appeared at the top of the stairs to see Miles trying to wave a small puff of smoke away from the top of a pot bubbling over the fireplace. He looked almost comedic, coughing and leaning over the pot while he tried to balance on his crutches.

"What did you do?" Letty laughed. She opened the window that looked out over Lantern Lane so the smoke would have a place to go.

"I was trying to make soup," Miles explained, "but as you can see, I didn't know what I was doing and left it on too long."

"It looks like you need some more practice," Letty teased good-naturedly. She was so glad to be able to make jokes with Miles instead of finding him moping around. Of course, it wasn't particularly surprising. Miles had never been one to mope, even in the most difficult of circumstances.

"I guess I do. Do you think it's salvageable?" Miles grabbed a spoon and dipped it into the pot, then brought it to his lips. Immediately, he winced. One eye squinted up, his lips puckered, and he started spluttering. "Nope," he choked. "I don't think that would be edible even if I hadn't burned it."

"It can't be that bad," Letty argued. She got a spoon of her own and tasted the soup, although she instantly regretted it. She had been wrong; it was just as bad as Miles had made it out to be. Letty didn't think she'd ever tasted more salt in a dish in her life. She couldn't help but laugh, nearly choking on the mouthful of salt-infested soup. She quickly filled a glass with water from the pitcher on the table and tried to wash the flavor out of her mouth.

"Why are you making soup to begin with?" Letty continued. "You've never done it before, have you?"

"I was trying to make it for Mama," Miles explained. The jovial tone in the room suddenly deflated. "I thought it might help her feel better. She hasn't felt well since we got the news about Papa. I don't think she's gotten out of bed at all."

"Oh." She had known that the happy mood wouldn't last forever, but she wished it had stayed a little while longer. "Is she sleeping?"

"She might be, but she won't mind being woken up. She'll be excited to see you."

Miles gestured for Letty to follow him back to their mother's bedroom, then tapped gently on the side of the doorframe. "Mama, I have a surprise for you," Miles said. Letty came around behind Miles and stood next to him.

Her mother sat up sleepily. It was immediately clear what Miles had been saying: Mama was pale in the face, and her eyes were swollen and watery. She likely had not been sleeping well, something Letty fully understood.

"Hi, Mama," she said. Seeing her mother in this condition left her almost breathless.

"Letty?" Mama replied. She scooted over and patted the open space on the bed next to her. Letty gladly ran to sit next to her mother.

"How are you feeling?" Letty asked as Mama took her daughter's hands in hers.

Mama smiled weakly. "Much better with my sweet girl home."

"That's not really an answer to my question, Mama," Letty chided.

Mama sighed and shifted in her bed. "Well, right now my heart is hurting, and that makes the rest of my body hurt."

"Will we always feel this way about losing him?" Letty asked.

Mama reached out a hand to stroke Letty's hair, and Letty moved from the bed to the floor, letting her head rest next to her mother.

"No, we won't always feel this way, and your father wouldn't want us to always feel this way. But I don't think we will ever stop missing him . . . or rejoicing in our memories of him."

Letty didn't enjoy the idea that she might never stop missing her father, but it made sense. In a way, it was almost comforting. It was better to keep him with her, if only in memory, than to lose him altogether.

"Letty," Miles whispered. "Why don't we finish getting Mama something to eat."

Letty looked back over her shoulder to see Miles still leaning against the doorframe with a small, red mark under each eye, as if he had rubbed tears away too quickly. Letty wondered if he had been thinking the same things she was. She turned back to look at Mama's face. Her eyes were closed now, and she leaned back in bed, breathing softly. Her fingers had stopped their constant movement, now resting still in Letty's hair. Letty reached her hand up and slowly, carefully removed Mama's hand from her head, placing it back on the bed. She stood quietly and tiptoed back to Miles.

The two sat quietly at the kitchen table for a moment, both lost in thought, neither sure how to break the peaceful silence. Finally, Miles hobbled over to the kitchen cabinets and began rummaging through them.

"What do we have for Mama to eat?" Letty asked. "Besides burnt salt soup, that is."

Miles chuckled. "There's plenty. One of the men from the search party gave us some cheese from the dairy farm just outside town, and Kiana—you know, the cobbler's wife—came by early this morning with a loaf of bread."

Letty's head snapped up. "She did?"

Miles looked over his shoulder with one eyebrow arched. "Yes," he said questioningly. "Why do you seem so surprised?"

"Did you hear about her husband?"

Miles turned fully around to face Letty and leaned back against the cabinets. He shook his head. "What are you talking about?"

"Her husband went missing two days ago. He went out to run errands and didn't come back."

Miles's eyes widened in shock, then narrowed as he thought

through it a bit. "Just like Papa," he mused, rapping his knuckles on the cabinet tops.

"Exactly." Letty traced her fingertips along the grains of the table for a moment, staring intently at the patterns she felt against her skin. "What do you think is going on, Miles?"

He shook his head, seemingly dumbfounded by this new revelation. "I don't know, but I don't like it, whatever it is."

Miles went back to preparing food for Mama, and silence once again enveloped the kitchen as both Miles and Letty considered any connections they could possibly find. Letty didn't manage to come up with any, and since Miles didn't speak up again, she assumed that he hadn't either.

When Miles had finished slicing and preparing the bread and cheese for Mama, Letty offered to take it to Mama's room so her brother wouldn't have to balance the plate while on his crutches. Just before she disappeared into the back room, Miles stopped her.

"Letty?" She turned her head at his voice. "There's no need to tell Mama about the cobbler yet. She's upset enough as it is."

Letty nodded slowly. Miles was right. When Mama got her strength back a bit, of course, they would tell her, but for now, it wouldn't do any good. Mama couldn't do much to help Kiana and her family in her condition, anyway. With that agreement between them, Letty drifted back to Mama's bedroom with lunch for her mother and a thousand questions floating in her head.

CHAPTER 9

Letty was glad Jocelyn had been so clear that she didn't need to be back at the castle immediately. All that day and the next, Letty brought food to Mama when she was awake and sat on the bed chatting about life at the castle while her mother ate. When Mama got tired, Letty left her to rest and sat at the kitchen table talking to Miles.

They had plenty of conversation to catch up on. The last time Letty had been home, it had been for such a short time that they hadn't had much of a chance to talk at all. Miles told her about his mishaps running the shop, and Letty explained the process of getting ready for the prince of Pelorias to come, noting the little smile that crossed his face whenever Jocelyn's name was mentioned. Mostly, they talked about Papa and Rylan the cobbler, and what possibly could have happened to both of them. They speculated that perhaps, for whatever reason, they had vanished into the dark forest to the south. It was the most logical explanation for a complete disappearance. After all, many travelers had faced that fate before the lights on Lantern Lane were erected to guide people away from the dangers of the forest. And yet, neither Letty nor Miles could imagine any reason they would have possibly gone to the forest, especially not the cobbler, who supposedly was simply running errands within the village when he went missing.

"What will happen to his family if he's not found?" Letty asked after they had discussed all of their wild—and not exactly logical—theories. "He and Kiana have four young children. How is she supposed to care for them without his help or the money from the cobbler shop?"

"I don't know, exactly," Miles said. "But thankfully, they live on Lantern Lane, and if there is anywhere that people will be taken care of, it's here. I mean, we don't even have small children to tend to, and look how well they've taken care of us. See how full our cupboards are? That's all from our neighbors."

Miles was right. Before Letty had even made it home the day before, half a dozen neighbors had brought baked goods, dairy products, and produce, and last night, someone had even come by with a pot of soup—a perfect replacement for Miles's ruined pot.

"If I weren't working at the castle, I could help watch Liam, Elsie, and the twins," Letty said, a slight pang of guilt tightening in her stomach.

"I know," Miles answered, "but someone else will help."

"Liam and Elsie won't have as much fun with them as they would with me." Letty smiled as she said it, mostly joking, but it was true that she had a special relationship with the children. She had often tended to them for a few hours on afternoons when Kiana needed extra help. Under any other circumstances, Letty wouldn't have had a second thought about offering that service.

"Maybe, but they're not difficult children to make happy," Miles countered. "Besides, you're doing good work at the castle, and the princess needs you there. I know I argued against it before, and I'm still not happy about it, but I know you're right to be doing what you feel you need to."

"Thank you," Letty said. Then, with a teasing smile, she added, "That change of heart wouldn't happen to have anything to do with you being sweet on Jocelyn, would it?"

"What? No!" Miles spluttered as his cheeks turned bright pink. "It's just that the more you talk about your work, the more I realize it seems good for you." Miles pushed his hand through his hair, moving the blond strands away from his face. "Besides, I am not sweet on Jocelyn. I've hardly even met her." He was still blushing though, and when Letty didn't answer, he looked up at her, chuckling at the grin on her face. "Fine, I think she is very pretty, and she seems kind from the stories you tell. But that's all. That does not mean I'm sweet on her."

"I suppose," Letty relented. "You're correct, you don't know her well enough for that . . . but I think you would be if you got to know her. She's 17, you know, only one year younger than you."

Miles laughed and ducked his head so that his forehead touched the table. "Can we please change the topic now?"

Letty walked across the room and slumped exaggeratedly against the window, the back of her hand to her forehead, pretending to faint as though the request was simply too much to ask. "I suppose so," she joked with a dramatic sigh. She had bumped her hurt shoulder leaning against the wall and turned her head to examine it as she rubbed the sore spot.

As Letty's head was turned, she caught a glimpse through the window slats of a very tall man walking along Lantern Lane. It reminded her of another story from the castle she had not told Miles about.

"What's the matter?" Miles asked, noticing the faraway look in her eyes as she stared out the window.

"Nothing, it's just that there's a man out there who reminded me of something . . ." She sat back, placing both palms on the table and staring intensely at Miles. He blinked quickly and drew back, caught off guard by her sudden change in demeanor, but he said nothing. Instead, he sat at attention, ready to hear whatever story Letty had to tell.

"When I was cleaning the guest bedrooms for the prince and his parents a few days ago, I looked out the window and saw a tall, thin man climb over the garden wall," Letty explained. Miles's eyebrows shot up his face.

"Did you tell anybody? Someone trespassing on the castle grounds could be a danger."

"I was going to," Letty replied, "but then someone else came to meet him." Miles nodded, encouraging her to go on. Letty shifted in her chair. She knew that the next part would sound bizarre, maybe even a bit unbelievable, but she knew what she had seen. "It was King Henrick."

Miles's face relaxed at that news. "Oh, I see. Well, if it was just a messenger for the king, then it's nothing to be worried about."

Letty squirmed. "I know, but something about it just didn't seem right. I mean, why did they meet out in the gardens instead of in the throne room or somewhere else in the castle? And the king was hidden in the shadow of the castle wall, always looking around like he was worried about being seen. Besides that, whatever they were talking about seemed heated. Everything about it was odd."

"That does sound odd," Miles agreed, "but I'm sure there was a perfectly reasonable explanation for it. He is the king, after all. He probably has to do a lot of things that you and I wouldn't understand."

Letty shrugged. She had to admit that Miles's explanation seemed logical, but she was going to need more convincing than that. In fact, the more she thought about it, the more off-putting it was: the man in the cloak, hiding his face as best he could, and the king emerging stealthily from the shadows. Their large, angry-looking movements were enough to tell Letty that something was unusual. She wasn't going to dismiss it quite as easily as Miles had.

"So, when are you going back?" Miles asked after a brief lull in the conversation.

"I don't know. It should be soon, but I don't want to leave you alone taking care of Mama like this. I'm worried about her."

"That makes sense—" Miles began. Before he could finish, creaking floorboards caught both of their attention.

Both Miles and Letty turned their heads instantly toward the noise, from the direction of the back room. Miles cocked an eyebrow and glanced at Letty as though questioning whether she heard the same thing he did.

"Mama, do you need help?" Miles called out.

Mama's somewhat strained voice responded, "No, I'm fine."

In unison, Miles and Letty pushed away from the table, and Letty went to Mama's bedroom while Miles thumped along behind.

When she passed through the doorway, Letty was stunned to see that her mother was no longer lying in bed. Instead, she was standing, one hand against the wall to maintain her balance. She was breathing a bit heavier than she normally would as she tried to battle against the weakness in her body, but she was moving, placing one shaky foot slowly in front of the other.

"What do you need, Mama? I can get it for you; you don't have to be up!" Letty said, rushing to Mama's side to help her back to bed.

"I don't need anything, I just wanted to come out and be with you and Miles. I'm stiff from sitting in that bed for two days. Besides, I'd like to join in your conversation."

With a shrug to Miles, Letty offered Mama her hand to lean on as she walked. She seated her mother at the kitchen table, made sure she was comfortable, and brought her a glass of water.

"So, Letty," Mama said once she was settled, "when *are* you going back?"

Letty and Miles cast sidelong glances at each other. Mama had clearly heard Miles's question all the way from the bedroom. What else had she heard? Had she heard Letty tell her brother she was worried about Mama? Could she have heard them talking about the missing cobbler?

"I don't know yet. Maybe in a few days?" Letty replied, trying to gauge what her mother had actually overheard and how she may have felt about it.

Mama tilted her head. "Do you really want to stay away that long?"

Letty hesitated. She wasn't sure. Did she? She loved being with her family, of course, but a large part of her longed to get back to the bustle of the castle and the controlled chaos of preparations for the prince. She missed having something to do, and the talks she had been having with Mama and Miles had helped her already. Her heart still ached, no question, but she felt far more capable of dealing with the heaviness than she had been previously. She had to consider her mother, though. Mama was still sick, and she would stay until Mama didn't need her help anymore.

Mama seemed to see every thought that floated through Letty's head. She smiled softly. "It's OK, Letty, you can go back. I'm going to get stronger, and I'll be all right. I don't need you to stay away from your work because of me. I want you to stay home only for as long as you need."

What a way Mama had of knowing exactly what her children needed to hear! "I'll go back tomorrow afternoon," Letty finally decided. "There are only a few days left until the prince comes from Pelorias, and I have responsibilities to take care of."

Mama smiled. "What a hard-working girl I have," she said. "So, what do you say we make a nice meal tonight and enjoy one another's company until Letty goes back to the castle?"

"I'll never say no to that," said Miles.

Mama helped with the cooking when she could, but she still needed to take frequent breaks to rest while she directed Miles and Letty in the kitchen. Letty went down to the root cellar for a pork belly while Miles and Mama began on the pastry dough to make meat pies—a rare treat considering the hours they took to assemble and bake. It was the perfect way to spend time together.

They barely let the pies cool before they ate them. By the time they had finished, Letty, Miles, and Mama were all tired from spending the afternoon in the hot kitchen. It was a good exhaustion, though, the kind that comes only after a joyful day, and Letty went to bed happier and calmer than she had been in quite some time.

CHAPTER 10

Mama fussed with Letty's lavender shawl, trying to get it to lay properly across Letty's shoulders as she prepared to return to the castle.

"Do you have everything you need?" Mama asked Letty for the second time since lunch.

"Yes, Mama. I didn't bring anything other than what I'm wearing," Letty said with a chuckle.

"Right, right. Well, be careful walking back to the castle, and come back soon, all right, my girl?"

"I will." Letty gave her mama a peck on the cheek, then turned to her brother.

"Can I take some candy from the shop for Liam and Elsie? I promised I'd bring them some on my way back."

"Of course," Miles quickly agreed. "In fact, you should bring a basket of groceries as well. I'm sure Kiana would appreciate it."

"That sounds nice," Mama chimed in. "Say hello to Kiana for me when you visit, won't you?"

"I will," Letty promised. Her response was a bit tense as she realized that Mama still didn't know the reason why Miles had suggested the act of service—as far as Letty knew, Mama was completely unaware of the cobbler's disappearance. "Miles, would you help me put the basket together?"

"Sure," Miles responded. He jammed his crutches under his arms and followed Letty down the stairs, intently focused on the steps so he wouldn't fall.

Down in the shop, Letty immediately grabbed her usual delivery basket, blowing a bit of newly accumulated dust out of the crevices before turning around to face Miles.

"Mama needs to know about Kiana's husband," she whispered. "She's a bit stronger now, and she's going to find out eventually whether we tell her or not."

"I know," said Miles in a low voice. "I'll tell her today, I promise. I just need to find the right time. It's not something I want to mention out of nowhere."

Letty nodded in agreement. She was glad they were on the same page, and, perhaps selfishly, she was glad not to be the one to have to tell Mama about the second missing man.

Letty took two lollipops from the large glass jars on the counter while Miles removed a few items from the shelves behind the register. Together, they piled the basket high with all of the usual staples—yeast, sugar, beans, and oats—plus a few special things like jelly and applesauce. Once the basket was as full as Miles and Letty could make it, Letty tucked the handle of the brimming basket into the crook of her left elbow like she always did. She wrapped her free arm around her brother's waist in a goodbye hug and called a farewell up the stairs to Mama. Then, with one last pat of her pockets to make sure the lollipops were secure inside, Letty headed out the door and back up Lantern Lane toward the cobbler's shop. Around the back of the little building she went, grinning at the sight of red gingham curtains in the window and the piles of sticks scattered around the backyard, left behind from whatever game

Liam and Elsie had been playing most recently. She rapped on the door and was met by a relieved-looking Kiana.

"You're an angel, Letty," she said as she eyed the basket on Letty's arm. "This is such an enormous help."

Liam and Elsie danced around Kiana's and Letty's legs as they unloaded the groceries, chattering away with constant little interruptions into Letty's conversation with their mother.

Suddenly, Elsie stopped jumping around and gasped. "Liam!" she shouted, then cupped her tiny hand around her brother's ear and whispered to him loudly. Liam grinned, and Elsie began bouncing again—this time up and down instead of in circles, sending the ribbons in her hair flying. "Can we go outside, Mammy?" Elsie asked.

"Don't you want to stay and talk to Letty?" Kiana asked.

"Yes," said Liam, "but first we want to go outside."

"All right, I suppose, but don't stay out too long. I'm sure Letty has to leave soon."

Liam nodded emphatically, and Elsie squealed as the two scampered out the door.

Letty chuckled. "What are those two up to?" she asked.

Kiana shook her head with a laugh. "I never know," she said. "They might be collecting rocks, they might be digging a trench. Who's to say?"

Letty and Kiana continued to make small talk while the children were outside, chatting about the castle as they finished putting the groceries away. After a few minutes, they were interrupted by the returning sounds of squeals and little thumping feet as Elsie and Liam approached the door.

"For Letty!" Elsie shouted.

"Look what we got you!" Liam added. Both children waved their hands in the air, each with their little fingers wrapped around the short stem of a flower.

"Oh, they're beautiful!" Letty said, crouching down to talk to the children. They thrust the flowers into Letty's hand, and her fingers fumbled to grasp the stubby stems as she studied the petals.

"Do you 'member them?" Elsie asked, struggling to pronounce such a big word.

"Winter roses," Letty mused, not looking up from the flowers as she turned them about in her hands. "I do remember."

An image came suddenly to Letty's mind from a few nights prior: another winter rosebush, this one next to the castle wall. It had been there that night when Miles told her that Papa was truly gone, after she had run into the garden. There was something unusual about that bush. What was it? She couldn't quite remember . . .

The window. There was a window next to the winter rosebush at the castle, a small, narrow window near the ground.

Was there something behind that window?

Letty shook her head. "I brought you something too," she said. She pulled the lollipops from her pocket with her free hand and placed them in Liam's and Elsie's waiting palms, completely forgetting the silly hiding games she usually played.

Elsie wrapped her tiny arms around Letty's neck and gave her a kiss on the cheek. "Thank you, Letty," she said.

Letty hugged her back, staring over the little girl's shoulder distractedly.

"I'm sorry, I've really got to go," Letty said, standing quickly. "Thank you for letting me stop by. If you need any other groceries, please go talk to Miles; he'll be happy to help you."

"Is everything all right?" Kiana's brow furrowed. "You look like you've seen a ghost."

"Everything is fine, I think," Letty replied. "I just remembered something, and I have to get back to the castle."

"Oh, I see. Well, get back safely!"

Letty smiled over her shoulder on her way out the door. "Thank you, Kiana," she said. "Bye-bye, Liam! Bye-bye, Elsie!" she added with a wiggle of her fingers.

"Bye-bye!" the children shouted in unison, waving wildly at her.

Letty stopped by the winter rosebush at the side of the house as she made her way back to the street. Yes, it looked exactly like the one against the castle wall; the memory was vivid. Letty had to get back to the castle and see what was hiding behind that window.

A light dusting of snow was starting to fall as Letty ran up Lantern Lane. She pulled her shawl tightly around her shoulders to keep it from blowing off, Liam and Elsie's flowers still clutched between her fingers.

Before she went inside the castle, Letty dashed around its side to the winter rosebush and, more importantly, the slim opening next to it. She crouched down beside it, trying to peer inside, but the bars were so close together that it was hard to see what was on the other side. Letty lay down flat on her stomach, ignoring the wet speckling of the few snowflakes on the ground against the fabric of her dress and the mild pang in her right shoulder. She squinted, straining to see through the bars on the opening.

No matter how close she got, the angle kept her from seeing the vast majority of the space. If she held her head in a very awkward position, she could see a small bit of the dirty floor directly below her. Otherwise, she could see little more than the ceiling of the room and a few patches of the upper wall illuminated by the dim light that filtered around her shadow. That seemed to be the only light in the room. No candles or lanterns flickered, and certainly no chandeliers hung there as they did in the rest of the castle.

"Hello?" Letty called softly through the opening. Her words reverberated off the walls, confirming that whatever this room was, it was sparsely furnished, if furnished at all. Still, she held her breath, listening intently for any response. Nothing came.

No, no! Letty thought. *There has to be someone in there. I wasn't just hearing voices the other night. I can't have been.*

She tried calling out one more time, just a bit louder. "Please, is anyone there?" The desperation she felt was apparent in the tightness of her voice. Once again, she remained perfectly still as she listened for an answer to her call.

There! There was some kind of noise coming from inside. She wasn't sure where it came from, exactly, but it was there—a breath, a squeak, a soft thud. Letty craned her neck, trying to find any position that would allow her to see more of the room. There was another sound, more distinct now: a scuttling noise, followed by a short series of squeaks. Suddenly, the source of the noise scampered directly beneath her through a tiny patch of light: a large rat, its feet scratching at the stone flooring as it ran.

Letty recoiled from the window in an instant. She hated rats. As she collected herself, she realized that it must have been the rat making the noise she had heard. The little thud, the squeaking—of course it had been a rat. Maybe there really wasn't anything—or anyone—else in there after all.

With one last tentative glance through the bars, Letty pushed herself up from the ground, shivered in disgust from the sight of the rodent, and made her way to the front of the castle to get back to her duties.

CHAPTER 11

The moment Letty entered the grand foyer, she was met by the sound of pandemonium spilling out from the open doors of the ballroom. Servants bustled in and out, and the sounds of scraping objects, along with dozens of voices, came from inside. Letty had intended to go straight upstairs to clean, but she couldn't help diverting to the ballroom instead.

A towering ladder stood in the middle of the ballroom, directly beneath the largest of the three chandeliers. A man balanced at the top of the ladder with a box of elegant taper candles resting precariously on the step next to him. One by one, he removed the used candles from their individual holders and replaced them with fresh ones, taking a polishing rag to a piece of gold or a dangling crystal as needed.

Beneath him, maids and footmen circled the perimeter of the ballroom adjusting small tables, inching them this way and that to ensure they were spaced properly. Other maids with small scrubbing brushes, dusters, and buckets of soapy water carefully inspected the walls, ensuring that any dirt or dust caught in the stone was thoroughly cleansed. All of them smiled and laughed as they chatted together. They seemed to be enjoying their preparations for the prince's arrival.

"Well, would you look at that? Letty is back!" called out one of the maids who sometimes joined Letty and Jocelyn at mealtimes.

Many of the faces in the ballroom turned and smiled at her, and a chorus of "Hello, Letty!" echoed from the friends and acquaintances she had made at the castle.

"Where is Princess Maisy?" Letty asked the maid who had first noticed her. "Usually the princess has her dancing lessons in here around now."

"She's in the kitchen with Jocelyn inspecting the most recent grocery purchase," the maid replied with an eye roll. "Truly, she must have changed the menu for next week three times already."

"Oh, dear," Letty said. She could picture the chaos that might be happening right now.

Give her the benefit of the doubt, Letty, she reminded herself. With a wave, she dismissed herself from the ballroom and made her way to the kitchen.

If the ballroom was pandemonium, the kitchen was complete and utter mayhem. Princess Maisy sat in the middle of the kitchen atop a high stool while kitchen hands dashed back and forth with fruits, vegetables, and meats in their arms, displaying them for the princess's approval before they put anything away in its proper place. Letty was afraid that she would find that the princess had reverted back to her old careless and arrogant ways, but instead, she found Princess Maisy smiling politely and directing everyone gracefully.

Letty cut her way through the bustling swarm toward Princess Maisy.

"Hello, Your Highness," Letty said as she approached. "What would you like me to do? I can work in the guest bedrooms, or I can help somewhere else if you would rather."

Princess Maisy turned and beamed as she realized who was speaking to her. "Letty, you're back! I wasn't sure when you would return, but I'm glad you're here. I hope you're feeling better." She sat up straighter as she changed the topic of conversation to address Letty's question. "If you'd like to work in the guest rooms for now, that would be fine. Tea is in about half an hour, so you won't be up there for long."

"Yes, Your Highness," Letty replied, then turned immediately to the door to begin.

After a few days at home, Letty felt more motivated than ever to do her duties well, and she got to work right away. She diligently scrubbed at every nook and cranny in the stone walls, just as the maids had been doing in the ballroom. She knew she wouldn't be able to finish scouring the entire room in the thirty minutes before tea, but considering how much dust buildup was on those walls, it seemed to Letty that it was a task worth starting on anyway. She started near the desk, making her way around as much of the room as she could in the time she was given.

Letty didn't mean to look out the window as she scrubbed the wall next to it. She was focused on her work and had no intention of distracting herself with whatever might be outside, but when a movement below caught her attention, Letty couldn't help but take a quick look. An eerie feeling settled over her as she realized she was watching a familiar scene. What was that tall man doing back in the gardens? Letty rubbed her eyes, thinking that perhaps this was a hallucination of some kind because she had been telling Miles the story just the day before. But when her eyes opened again, the man was still there, right at the bottom of the garden wall, which Letty presumed he had just climbed over as she had seen the time before.

She craned her neck, trying to see if the king were waiting again in the shadow of the castle. Sure enough, there he stood, waiting for the intruder to join him.

Perhaps the tall man could feel Letty's eyes on him, because the next moment, he looked up directly at the window Letty was watching from. She twisted away from the window as quickly as she could, pressing her back firmly against the wall and praying that the man hadn't seen her. She could almost hear Miles's voice telling her the king was free to meet with whomever he wanted and that Letty didn't need to concern herself with it. He would insist that everything was perfectly fine. But if that were really the case, why didn't it *feel* perfectly fine? Why was Letty's heart pounding, and why couldn't she quite catch her breath? It made absolutely no sense to be so afraid of being seen, but she was.

Slowly—very slowly—Letty poked her head out from her hiding spot to see if the tall man was still looking up at her. Thankfully, he must not have seen her because he had moved on. He was now standing with the king near the castle wall.

Eavesdropping was wrong, Letty knew, but she reasoned that she was just trying to affirm she had no reason to worry. As gently as she could, Letty placed both of her hands against the windowpane and pushed, allowing it to swing open ever so slightly. The window creaked as it moved. Letty winced and held her breath, but neither the king nor his tall visitor seemed to notice.

The two men stood quite close together, and although their gestures and expressions were once again animated, their voices were hardly above a low murmur. Letty could hear very little, but every once in a while, one or two words would float through the window to her: "Princess . . . maps . . . gold . . . soon." Try as she might, Letty couldn't hear anything between those words. When it seemed that their conversation had finished, the tall man took another worried glance around and slunk back to the garden wall he had just come from.

Letty certainly did not feel any better about the tall man and the king than she had when she told Miles about the first time she saw them. Although none of the words she heard from them were inherently concerning, they weren't necessarily comforting, either. What could they possibly have been talking about? Miles would tell her it probably didn't matter, but what if it did?

On her way to tea, she passed by the winter rosebush without stopping, hoping not to see the rat she had thought was a person. She briefly considered running around to the other side of the castle to examine the spot where King Henrick and the tall man had met, but she knew she wouldn't find anything there. If they had dropped anything or left clues of some sort behind, Letty would have been able to see them from the window.

Princess Maisy had worries of her own, and they were vastly different from Letty's concerns about the king and the tall, mysterious visitor. Letty welcomed the distraction that came from discussing Princess Maisy's guest list for the ball, fretting about which nobles had responded to their invitations and whether anyone else should be invited. "This is an important event," Princess Maisy explained, "and I want only the most respectable people in attendance. The help for the evening also must be selected carefully. I want to make sure that only the most presentable and skilled staff will be serving at the ball."

Letty hadn't considered that last aspect. Suddenly, she wondered if it would be possible for her to be selected to serve. She hoped so;

it would be wonderful to see the ball's splendor and watch the results of everyone's hard work.

Once tea was over, Letty spent the rest of the afternoon and most of the evening bouncing back and forth between the tasks that Jocelyn and the other maids were assigned and moving between the ballroom, the grand entry, and the kitchen to help with whatever odds and ends she could.

Just as the princess had been, all the maids were abuzz with the idea of the ball. Some were chattering about specific nobles they had heard would be in attendance, while others swooned over how beautiful and extravagant it would be. Still others discussed how much they hoped they would be allowed to serve drinks or hors d'oeuvres so they could observe everything and everyone, just as Letty had been wishing.

Letty let her imagination wander as she worked, picturing herself serving noblemen and ladies, listening to the grand music, and admiring the gowns and fine suits that everyone would be wearing.

By the time Princess Maisy was ready for bed at nine o'clock, Letty was thoroughly exhausted. Considering her unproductive visit to the rosebush window, her worry over what she had seen from the guest bedroom, and every bit of spare mental space being taken up with the ball and the guest list and who would be serving, it had been a mentally exhausting day. After adding all that to the physical work of cleaning, she truly could not wait to drop into bed and fall into a deep sleep.

When Letty at last arrived in her room, something large was on her bed. *That is odd*, she thought. *I don't remember leaving anything there.* Curiously, Letty crept closer to investigate but stopped in surprise once she realized what it was: a stunning turquoise gown with delicate floral appliqués down the front. The full skirt and short sleeves were lightly ruffled and fluttery. Letty remembered this gown—it was the ball gown the seamstress had initially designed for Princess Maisy and the only one the princess had asked the seamstress to scrap after her apology. Letty had assumed they would simply take apart the rejected ball gown. What was it doing lying on her bed?

Letty ran her fingers over the floral designs and rubbed the light, flowy fabric on the sleeves between her fingers. There was a slip of paper on the shoulder, attached to the fabric with a pin. Letty removed the pin and held the note closer to her face so she could read the small, elegant print.

Dear Letty, it read,

I am so sorry to hear about your father. I am not good at talking about these things, but I would like to do something for you. I am pleased to formally invite you to attend the ball at the end of the coming week—as a guest, not as a servant. Your speedy reply is requested and appreciated.

Cordially, Princess Maisy

Letty stood in stunned contemplation for a moment. This couldn't be real, could it? Before she knew what she was doing, Letty flew down the hall, barely tapping on the princess's door before flinging it open, startling Princess Maisy out of the book she was reading.

"Is this serious?" Letty still had the note clutched in her hand, and she held it up to show Princess Maisy.

"The invitation?" Princess Maisy asked. She tried to suppress a smile as she slowly and calmly placed a bookmark between the pages of her novel and set it to the side. "Yes, it is a perfectly legitimate invitation. Do you accept?"

Letty felt her eyes filling with tears as she stood in the doorway. It might have been a silly thing to be emotional over, but the guest list was so important to Princess Maisy, and she had spent so much time discussing it. If she wanted Letty to be on that guest list, it was one of the most sincere gifts she could offer.

"I would love to," Letty stammered. "Thank you."

Princess Maisy extended her hand, and after a moment's hesitation, Letty approached and took it. Princess Maisy placed her other hand on top of Letty's comfortingly.

"I know a ball can't take away the pain you're feeling right now." She choked up as she said it, and Letty wondered if the princess was remembering the loss of her own parents. "But I figured it was the least I could do. Besides, you've been such a help. You deserve to be there."

Letty didn't know how to respond. She tried to form words, but none came out, leaving her mouth gaping. After a moment, Princess Maisy laughed.

"You can go if you'd like. You don't have to say anything else."

Letty nodded and made her way back to the door. "Thank you," she said one more time before she left.

Princess Maisy smiled at her and nodded gracefully as she picked her book back up.

Letty leaned against the door once it closed behind her and laughed quietly to herself for a moment in pure disbelief. *This is incredible*, she thought. *I am going to the ball!*

CHAPTER 12

The next three days flew by faster than any Letty had ever experienced. By the time her head hit the pillow each night, she could hardly remember what she had done that morning. Her bustling days were filled with sitting in on final fittings for the princess's gowns, helping the maids with their cleaning, and perfecting almost every part of the guest bedrooms for the king, queen, and prince of Pelorias. The artwork was the only thing left to take care of—it would be the finishing touch and make the rooms seem welcoming and comfortable. While Letty had been visiting home, Jocelyn found a painter in a nearby village who provided art pieces for the bedrooms. And so, with one day left until the prince arrived, Letty, Jocelyn, and Jacob, the footman, stood in the first guest bedroom to hang the artwork. That morning, Jacob had used a drill and an auger to make a hole in the wall where a sturdy peg could be placed to hang the picture, and all that was left was to lift the painting onto the peg.

"Jocelyn is going to have to watch to make sure it's level," Jacob said as the three of them stared at the large seaside painting leaning against the wall. "She won't be able to reach high enough to get the painting on the peg." There was teasing in his voice, but he was right; Jocelyn was far too short to do the job. "Letty, come take the other side," Jacob continued. Letty shrugged in agreement and stood on one side of the painting while Jacob stood on the other.

"I don't know. Maybe we should go get another footman," Jocelyn said skeptically. "It looks really heavy. Are you sure you can lift it, Letty?"

Jacob shook his head, and one corner of his mouth turned up. "I think she'll be all right. You're strong, aren't you?" he asked Letty.

For a moment, Letty thought maybe Jocelyn was right and they should get another footman, but Jacob's comment made her pause. Of course she was strong! Besides, the painting didn't look *that* heavy. She was sure that with Jacob's help, she could hang it up perfectly fine.

"Don't worry, Jocelyn, I can lift it," Letty insisted.

"I thought so," said Jacob. Jocelyn still looked apprehensive at the idea, but Letty ignored that and got ready to move ahead with the plan anyway.

"Lift with your legs, Letty," Jacob advised as they both bent down. Letty placed her hands at the bottom of the frame and braced herself to lift.

"Ready," she grunted.

"On three," Jacob said. "One . . . two . . . three!"

Letty and Jacob lifted quickly, and the painting was up to waist height in an instant. Letty heard a small pop, and her shoulder stung a bit, but she ignored it; her shoulder had been feeling much better over the last few days so she wasn't particularly worried.

"Still doing OK over there?" Jacob asked around the painting.

"Yes," Letty replied through her teeth, "let's just hurry with this."

"Sounds good. We've got to get it up a little higher, then," he said.

Letty heaved again and managed to get the picture up to about her chest level before a shooting pain jolted through her shoulder and down her arm. The sharp sensation shocked Letty, and without thinking, her hands slipped out from underneath the painting. She jumped back instinctively, yelping and clutching her shoulder.

"Whoa!" Jacob shouted. He wobbled forward and back, trying to compensate for the sudden absence of support on the other side, but no matter how much he adjusted his grip, he couldn't save the painting from crashing to the ground with a catastrophic splintering sound.

"Letty! What did you do?" Jacob shouted as he set the other side of the painting down as gently as he could.

"Letty! Are you all right?" Jocelyn cried at the same time. She rushed to Letty's side.

Letty leaned against the wall and gritted her teeth against the pain. It was sharper than it had been when she first fell trying to hang the drapes a few days prior.

"Just give me a minute," Letty groaned.

"What just happened?" Jacob asked sharply. He seemed to be trying very hard to keep the edge out of his voice, but he wasn't particularly successful.

"Let her catch her breath, please, Jacob," Jocelyn chided.

Letty took a few slow, deep breaths, trying to fight back the hot tears threatening to escape her eyes. The sharp pain had dulled into an intense throbbing sensation.

"Last week, when I was hanging the new drapes over there, I fell and hurt my shoulder," Letty explained. "It's been feeling much better the last few days, but I guess it wasn't healed enough to lift something that heavy."

Jacob sighed deeply and put a hand to his forehead. "I wish you would have just said so. That could have saved your shoulder *and* the painting."

Dazedly, Letty's eyes wandered to where the painting was once again leaning against the wall, slightly lopsided now. She gasped as she realized the reason for the unevenness. The bottom corner of the frame on the side Letty had been carrying was completely shattered, and slivers of mahogany lay scattered around the frame. A few splinters had even shot upward and scratched at the painting, tainting the bright blues and greens on the canvas.

"Oh no," Letty whispered. "Oh no, oh no." The tears of pain Letty had been managing to hold back were now combined with tears of frustration, and she couldn't contain them anymore. She had ruined the painting! And what was worse, the prince would be arriving tomorrow. There was no time to replace it.

"Don't worry about it. I'm going to go find the princess," Jacob said, although he still sounded frustrated. "We need her input on what she wants done now."

Jacob quickly made his way out of the room, and Letty slumped against the wall again.

"Princess Maisy is going to be furious," she sniffled. "That was so foolish of me. I should have just let you go get a footman. Now I've ruined everything."

"It's all right, Letty, the princess will understand. Accidents happen." Jocelyn tried to comfort Letty, squeezing her arm soothingly.

Letty winced. Jocelyn seemed to have forgotten that the arm she had squeezed was the injured one.

"Oh! I'm so sorry," Jocelyn said upon seeing her grimace. She withdrew her hand. "How is your arm?"

"It hurts," Letty admitted, "but I still shouldn't have dropped the painting. What are we going to do now?"

"We'll probably just have a guest room without a painting. It isn't the end of the world."

Letty used her good hand to angrily wipe her tears. Maybe Jocelyn was right, but that didn't mean Letty felt any better about it. The timing couldn't have been worse, and as kind as Princess Maisy had been recently, Letty was sure that she would still be extremely upset.

Letty straightened at the sound of two or three sets of footsteps coming down the hall. "I can't believe this," came Princess Maisy's muffled voice from the other side of the door. The door swung open, and in came Princess Maisy, Jacob, and the head of staff.

The princess's eyes were drawn immediately to the artwork on the floor. She drew in a deep breath like she was gathering enough air to begin shouting, but just before she could, her eyes shifted over to Letty, who was standing hunched, puffy-eyed, and still grasping her shoulder.

"I'm so sorry, Your Highness," Letty said softly. "I didn't mean to. I was trying to help hang the painting, and then my shoulder . . . and it, it fell . . ." A lump rose in her throat, making it difficult for Letty to finish her thoughts.

Princess Maisy held her breath as Letty spoke. After a moment she slowly released it, her shoulders dipping as she did. She put her hands up in front of her.

"Well then," Princess Maisy said. "Letty, is your shoulder hurt?"

Letty blinked in surprise. She hadn't expected that to be the princess's first question.

"She could use some medical attention," Jocelyn jumped in while Letty hesitated.

"Of course. Jacob, go fetch a doctor, please," Princess Maisy instructed with a wave of her hand, then turned to the head of staff. "Marla, why don't you go down to the kitchen and make sure everything is in order there? I'll find you when I'm ready, and we can finish finalizing the last details for tomorrow."

Marla nodded and swiftly left to carry out the princess's request.

"Your Highness, aren't you angry?" Letty asked.

"Oh, of course I'm frustrated, but decorating concerns can wait until you've had your shoulder examined."

"See? I told you it would be OK," Jocelyn muttered.

The doctor arrived about forty minutes later and came straight upstairs to where Letty, Jocelyn, and Princess Maisy were waiting.

"Hello there, miss, I'm Dr. Barnett. I hear there's a problem with your shoulder. May I take a look?" the doctor asked.

"Yes—it's the right one," Letty said. She and Jocelyn were sitting on the edge of the bed now, while Princess Maisy had insisted on sitting in the desk chair. Dr. Barnett set his big black bag on the bed next to Letty.

"I need to check for swelling. Is that all right?"

Letty nodded, and the doctor gently examined her shoulder for any issues.

"I am feeling a lot of swelling," Dr. Barnett confirmed, "but the joint is still just where it should be—no dislocation, which was my biggest concern."

"What should I do?" Letty asked.

"Well, it seems to be a mild strain, so it will hurt for a while, but you should be able to move it normally in one to two weeks as long as you take care of it. I recommend keeping it in a sling and avoiding movement until it feels better."

"I think I can do that."

Jocelyn jumped up from her place at the end of the bed. "I'll go get some spare material from the seamstress's workshop to make a sling," she offered.

"Excellent. In that case, I'll be on my way to my next patient," said the doctor. "Send for me if there isn't any improvement within the next few days."

"Yes, sir. Thank you," Letty said.

Jocelyn and Dr. Barnett left at the same time, leaving Princess Maisy and Letty alone.

"I really am sorry, Your Highness," Letty said. "What do you want to do about the painting?"

"We'll simply have to do without it," Princess Maisy replied with a shrug. "I assume we still have art for the other two bedrooms, so we'll put the prince and his mother and father in those two rooms and have their servant stay in this one."

"Really?" Letty asked.

"Yes, really. Someone once told me that I need to stop worrying so much about making everything perfect and think more about understanding people. Or something like that. So as frustrated as I may feel when something like this happens, I'm going to try to let it go."

Letty grinned, and the princess cleared her throat.

"Now, if you'll excuse me," Princess Maisy said as she stood, "I've got to go find Marla."

CHAPTER 13

Princess Maisy exhaled deeply as Jocelyn fastened the last of the miniature buttons on the princess's elegant raspberry-colored chiffon dress. Letty watched from her perch on a stool, her right arm resting in the sling Dr. Barnett had recommended. Princess Maisy was facing Letty, and she brushed her hands over the front of the skirt nervously and fidgeted with the flowing sleeves.

"Does it look good?" Princess Maisy asked.

"You look wonderful," Letty smiled, admiring the perfect fit of the gown. "You should turn around and look in the mirror."

Princess Maisy gave a shallow nod as she turned slowly to the mirror. She ran her fingers through her ink-black curls, pulling them in front of her shoulders as she examined herself.

The seamstresses knew exactly what they were doing when they designed that dress: the vivid color stood out beautifully against Princess Maisy's pale skin and dark hair, and the full skirt and flowing sleeves were feminine and elegant. A delicate silver necklace and dainty earrings added an exquisite finishing touch to the overall appearance of her outfit. Letty grinned as she watched Princess Maisy's face settle into a calm confidence in the mirror. She could not have looked more perfect to meet the prince.

If Letty leaned to the side a bit, she could see herself in the mirror, too, and while she didn't look nearly as fancy as Princess

Maisy did, she had to admit that she was pleased with what she saw. Her favorite green dress had been freshly pressed, and the white embroidery added texture and detail. She had washed and styled her hair carefully to create the perfect ringlets and styled the top section in a cascading waterfall braid that she had tied back with a green ribbon, which stood out beautifully against her brown curls. The color of her dress matched her eyes perfectly, and the excitement of the day had brought a rosy glow to her cheeks. Her bright red sling was the only thing that didn't quite match, but Letty didn't care much; there were far bigger things to think about today.

"I feel like I'm forgetting something. What am I missing?" Princess Maisy said in a fluster.

"Everything is just right, Your Highness," Letty assured her. "The prince will think you're lovely, and he will appreciate the immense effort and planning you've put into everything. Stop worrying and just enjoy it!"

Princess Maisy sighed and put her hands up in surrender. "You're right, you're right." Then, she gasped. "No, wait! You're wrong. I am forgetting something." She rushed over to her armoire and tried to reach the top shelf, but she was just barely too short. "Letty, can you help?" she asked.

Letty laughed. "Sure." She walked over to the armoire and reached up with her left arm.

"Just that box on the shelf," Princess Maisy said.

Letty's fingertips barely managed to graze the box, but after a few tries, she scooched it close enough to the edge to pull it down.

"Be ready to catch it if it falls; I only have one hand at the moment," Letty warned the princess.

"No, no, I'll take it from here. It's close enough to the edge now that I can reach it, and I'd rather not risk a fall."

Letty stepped aside to let Princess Maisy finish retrieving her box from the shelf. The princess took the small wooden box in her hands, and Jocelyn shuffled closer, craning her neck and looking at the box inquisitively. Princess Maisy gently worked her fingers under the lid and pried it up.

Letty gasped as she looked into the box. A red satin cushion lay in the bottom, and on top of it rested a glittering silver crown. It was larger and more elaborate than the tiara Princess Maisy had been wearing the day Letty met her, and it was set all around with dozens of diamonds in various sizes and shapes.

"I'll wear this all the time when I become queen someday," Princess Maisy explained, sounding almost bashful. "For now, it's only for special occasions."

"It's beautiful," Letty sighed. "You should put it on."

Princess Maisy went back to her mirror and set the crown softly atop her black hair. The sunlight coming through the windows glittered off the surface of the gems, sending tiny rainbows dancing around the room.

"Wow," Letty and Jocelyn breathed in unison.

"There," Princess Maisy said with a smile and a nod. "Now I'm ready."

There was a tapping at the door, and Marla, the head of staff, opened the door.

"Your Highness," she said, "King Henrick would like to see you in the throne room."

Princess Maisy's smile fell, and she began fidgeting with her dress again. "Oh, all right," she said nervously. "Right now?"

"Yes, Your Highness. Before the prince arrives."

"Right, of course," Princess Maisy said, relaxing her shoulders with forced concentration. "Thank you, Marla."

Marla nodded and ducked out of the room. Princess Maisy took a deep breath, glanced once more in the mirror, and adjusted her crown slightly.

"Letty," the princess said, trying to sound nonchalant but failing, with her voice just above a whisper. "Would you mind coming with me?"

Letty's eyebrows rose. "You mean to see the king? Will he allow that?"

Princess Maisy waved her hand dismissively. "You're my lady-in-waiting. As long as I want you there, you can come with me basically anywhere. Besides, my uncle . . . well, he's very anxious about this visit, and he isn't very nice when he's that way. I don't want to talk to him alone."

Poor princess, Letty thought. *I can't imagine being that nervous around the person who raised you.*

"Yes," Letty agreed. "I'll come with you, don't worry. Are you ready?"

Princess Maisy nodded, relief crossing her face. "Let's go."

Letty and Princess Maisy made their way down the hall and the grand staircase. Two guards stood erect in front of the doors to the throne room, which Letty presumed meant the king was already waiting inside.

"Your Highness," one of them acknowledged the princess in a deep, gravelly voice. He and his partner each took hold of one of the well-polished handles and pulled the massive doors open.

"Just stay behind me," Princess Maisy whispered out of the

corner of her mouth as the doors opened. Letty quickly scampered behind the princess.

As the immense interior of the throne room became visible over Princess Maisy's shoulder, Letty remembered the brief glimpse she had gotten on her first day at the castle while she looked for the kitchen. The throne room appeared nearly identical to how she remembered it: the narrow red-and-gold carpet was still bright, magnificent, and plush beneath her feet, and the solid-gold throne still brilliantly shone. The only true difference was that the throne was not empty as it had been that first day. Now, King Henrick sat upon the throne, tall and regal. A golden crown rested atop his head, nestled against his thick, dark hair. His stony face was set in a firm, disapproving frown, and his gray-streaked beard was neatly trimmed and styled. He wore a white silk tunic with gold stitching and embroidery and a deep blue cape clasped just beneath his throat. The elegance of his clothing demonstrated the importance of the visiting royalty who would be arriving soon.

"What is that girl doing here?" King Henrick barked.

"This is Letty, my lady-in-waiting," Princess Maisy responded, gesturing behind her. "I believe you've met before."

"But why is she standing in my throne room? I don't recall inviting her."

"I—I asked her to join me. I would like to have her here to help me remember any important details or information you might mention." Princess Maisy stood tall and confident, but her voice shook slightly as she spoke.

"I should think you are capable of remembering things on your own, Maisy," he said. "If you're not, perhaps you are not ready to court the prince." Princess Maisy hung her head, and King Henrick rolled his eyes. "But I suppose the scrawny thing can stay if she's already here."

Letty did her very best to keep her face neutral. The king had made a similar comment about her before—on the day everyone found out the prince would be coming. Letty was shocked that an adult, much less a king, would be so unkind as to say something like that to a person's face.

"Now, I would just like to remind you, Maisy, how crucial these next three days will be," he said. "By the conclusion of this visit, I expect you to be betrothed to the prince of Pelorias, so you *must* make a good impression."

"I understand," Princess Maisy replied. Letty admired how solidly the princess spoke.

"I'm not certain you do," said the king. "Especially if this is the clothing you've chosen to greet him in."

This time, Letty couldn't keep her eyes from widening a bit. Why was he being so rude? She dipped her head so he could not see her facial expression.

"You will wait upstairs when the royal family arrives, and I will greet them. You shall meet the prince when I send for you," he explained. "You must impress the prince in every way. You must behave pleasantly toward him at all times. I understand that may be difficult for you, but no prince desires to be betrothed to an unpleasant princess."

"I don't expect that it will be difficult to be pleasant," Princess Maisy said. Letty noted that her hands, which remained firmly by her side, were clenched into tight fists. "I understand what you expect of me, Uncle."

King Henrick waved his hand. "You are dismissed. Go."

Princess Maisy gave a shallow curtsy, and Letty followed suit. Then they both turned and exited the throne room.

"I will be pleasant," Princess Maisy muttered as the doors closed behind her and Letty. "I am perfectly capable of impressing the prince. Aren't I?" She tossed her head and turned to Letty as she spoke the last question.

"Of course you are," Letty assured her. "You have a kind heart, you are gracious, and you've gotten good at showing it through practice. That is the most important thing. And on top of that, you are beautiful, intelligent, and talented in so many ways. The prince should be happy he is allowed to court you. You will be just fine."

Princess Maisy's eyes seemed to well a bit with tears. "Thank you, Letty. You're right; it will be fine. And if the prince decides he does not want to be betrothed to me, there are other princes from other kingdoms," she reasoned.

"Exactly," said Letty. "Now come, we can wait upstairs until the prince arrives."

Princess Maisy nodded, and as she and Letty continued their ascent back up the grand staircase, the doors of the grand entry suddenly opened behind them. Elias, the stable boy, came sprinting like a wild colt into the grand entry, panting.

"They're here!" he shouted. "I saw the carriage! The king, the queen, and the prince—they've arrived!"

CHAPTER 14

Princess Maisy paced back and forth across the library floor wringing her hands and readjusting her gown and jewelry. She had decided she preferred to wait in the library rather than her bedroom, while King Henrick welcomed the king, queen, and prince of Pelorias to the castle.

"Why don't you find something to read, Your Highness?" Letty suggested after a few minutes of the princess's pacing. "It might help you calm down." Letty was trying to remain calm herself, but the more Princess Maisy paced and twisted her hands, the more nervous Letty felt too.

"No, no, I couldn't," the princess muttered. "I can't sit still. I just don't know why they're taking so long."

"We've only been waiting five minutes, Your Highness," Letty pointed out. "They may still be getting out of their carriage."

Princess Maisy paused her back-and-forth across the floor and sighed. "You're right. I'll be patient." She nodded resolutely, then went immediately back to pacing.

Letty couldn't stand the constant soft thudding of Princess Maisy's shoes against the carpet or the tension and nervousness that filled the usually peaceful library. "I have an idea," she blurted at last. She didn't know what the idea was yet, but she would come up with something to create a bit of levity.

Princess Maisy turned to look at her inquisitively.

"I think we should practice," Letty went on, speaking as soon as the thought came to her mind.

"Practice?"

"Yes. I'll be the prince, and you be—well, you—and you can practice meeting him."

Princess Maisy's nervous frown turned into a hesitant smile, then a small giggle. "That's a peculiar idea, Letty," she said, "but let's try it since we're waiting anyway."

Letty faced the princess and cleared her throat. She straightened her posture to make herself as tall as she could, pulled her shoulders back, and put on a false deep voice.

"Your Highness," Letty rumbled. Her right arm was still in its sling, but her left arm swung out in a sweeping gesture to exaggerate a deep bow.

Princess Maisy laughed, then cleared her own throat and curtsied. "How do you do," she said. She daintily extended her hand as she would to the actual prince, and Letty took it and bowed again.

"I must say, Your Highness, that you look absolutely lovely." Letty's chin tilted into her chest as she tried to maintain her low voice.

"Why, thank you, sir, you are quite dapper yourself." Princess Maisy's lips puckered as she tried to keep a straight face.

Letty tried to think of what else a prince might do, but having never met a prince, she couldn't think to do anything except bow again, so deeply that her nose nearly touched her own knees.

"I have never been to Pelorias before, but I've heard it's lovely," Princess Maisy said, prompting Letty to continue the spontaneous

game of make-believe.

"Ah, of course. Here, I'll show you on the map." Letty removed a crisp rolled map from the shelf, pulled the end of the cord tied around it, and spread it across the table. She quickly located Pelorias on the map and pointed to the center. "Now this," Letty said dramatically, "is my . . ."

Letty trailed off as she turned to look at Princess Maisy. The princess's head was cocked to one side, her eyes fixated on a spot of the map off to the right of Letty's finger. One of her eyebrows arched slightly, and she leaned in toward the map.

"Is something the matter?" Letty asked, abandoning her false deep voice.

"It's nothing," Princess Maisy said with a shake of her head. "The mapmaker must have made a little mistake, that's all."

Letty squinted, trying to see what the princess could be talking about.

Princess Maisy pointed to a mountain range along Trielle's southern border. "These mountains," she explained. "I suppose I could be wrong, but I think they belong to Alria. On most maps, Trielle's border is at the base of these mountains. This map shows the border on the other side."

Letty was impressed that the princess remembered such details so well, but the difference didn't seem particularly notable to her.

"That is an odd mistake," Letty said with a shrug.

"Mhmm." Princess Maisy leaned further over the map, getting a closer look.

Just then, the library doors opened, and Marla, the head of staff, poked her head into the room. Princess Maisy snapped up at the sound.

"Your Highness, they're ready for you," Marla said.

Princess Maisy whipped around to look at Letty. Letty could see the worry swimming in the princess's eyes.

"You're coming with me, aren't you?" she asked.

Letty's eyes widened in surprise. "I can't meet the prince—not right now, anyway, not with you."

"But I feel calmer when you're there. Feel my hands. They're trembling. I need you nearby."

"Letty could wait at the top of the stairs," Marla suggested.

"Yes, yes, that's fine," Princess Maisy said. "Please, Letty, will you watch from the stairs?"

Letty knew it would be a bit awkward, but if that was what needed to happen to get Princess Maisy out of the library, then she would do it. "Of course I will. Now hurry; you can't keep the prince waiting."

With a grateful little smile, Princess Maisy nodded and turned to leave.

"Oh, wait!" Letty cried. "Let me straighten your crown." Letty adjusted Princess Maisy's crown, which had tilted off-center when they were examining the map. "There, now you're ready."

Princess Maisy exhaled slowly and deeply. "All right, let's go."

Letty had to admit that even she was a bit nervous. She brushed off the front of her dress and took a deep breath herself before following Princess Maisy out of the library. Princess Maisy walked so slowly it was almost painful for Letty to watch—she would much rather speed the process along and get it over with. Eventually, the princess reached the top of the stairs, and Letty stood just behind her, off to the side. The princess laid her hand gracefully at the top of the banister, and her raspberry-colored gown billowed out ever so slightly behind her. Letty couldn't see beyond Princess Maisy from her position, but she could hear everything perfectly.

"May I introduce my niece, Princess Maisy," came King Henrick's voice from the grand entry. "Princess, allow me to introduce King Dorian of Pelorias, along with his wife, Queen Adelaide, and of course, their son, Prince Cassius."

Princess Maisy's free hand bent gently at the wrist as it rested by her side, and she crossed one foot behind her before dipping into a deep, slow curtsy. The castle itself seemed to hold its breath as every eye was fixed on the princess. She held her curtsy for a long moment, showing the deepest respect for her visitors, then stood and began slowly down the stairs.

Letty moved slightly forward, just a bit closer to the stairs, so she could see below as Princess Maisy floated down the staircase.

The small group of royals stood exactly in the center of the grand entry as they waited for Princess Maisy to join them. King Henrick stood on the left end of the group, and next to him stood the man Letty presumed was King Dorian. He wore a scarlet cape over his black tunic and a golden crown set with red gemstones. He was short and slender, barely higher than King Henrick's shoulder. Queen Adelaide, at his side, towered over him, perhaps even an inch or two taller than King Henrick. Her light blonde hair was twisted into a complicated plaited updo and topped with a crown similar to her husband's. She wore a black-and-scarlet gown, matching the colors King Dorian was wearing. Beside her, on the far right of the group, stood Prince Cassius. He looked very much like his mother—tall with perfectly straight blond hair, a strong jaw, and brown eyes. He was dressed more simply than either his father or King Henrick, but he still looked regal in a red jacket with golden epaulets on the shoulders and a white sash across his torso. His black boots were polished to a perfect shine, and, of course, his head was adorned with a crown much like his father's.

Princess Maisy curtsied again when she reached the bottom of the stairs and extended her hand to Prince Cassius, as she had done while practicing with Letty. "How do you do, Your Highness?" she asked.

Prince Cassius bowed and took the princess's hand lightly in greeting. "How do you do, Princess? My father, mother, and I thank you for a warm welcome to your beautiful kingdom." His consonants were emphasized slightly, just like Jocelyn's were—a Pelorian accent, Letty realized. It made sense. After all, Jocelyn had told her that she had lived in Pelorias as a child.

"We are grateful that you could join us." Princess Maisy turned to King Dorian and Queen Adelaide. "Welcome to Trielle, Your Majesties. I'm sure you're exhausted from your travels. Would you like to see your bedrooms and rest for awhile, or would you prefer to stroll through the gardens until luncheon?"

"I, for one, would like to freshen up a bit," Queen Adelaide volunteered.

"Excellent," King Henrick said. "We'll have someone take you to your room and bring your trunks in from your carriage. Meanwhile, the prince and princess can spend some time in the garden while I take King Dorian on a tour of the castle."

"Wonderful plan," King Dorian agreed.

King Henrick gestured passively to Letty at the top of the stairs. "Maisy, have that girl show Queen Adelaide to her bedroom. King Dorian, if you'll follow me, I thought we would start in the armory on the third floor." King Henrick made his way up the stairs, and

King Dorian followed closely behind. Letty curtsied as the two kings passed her by, but neither of them paid her any mind. Princess Maisy turned over her shoulder and waved for Letty to join her in the grand entry, and Letty hurried down the stairs to the princess's side.

"Your Highness," Princess Maisy said to Prince Cassius. "Your Majesty," she addressed the queen. "This is my lady-in-waiting, Letty. Letty, would you please show Queen Adelaide to her bedroom?"

"Yes, of course," Letty said. "Your Majesty, right this way."

Neither Queen Adelaide nor Prince Cassius said a word to Letty during the introduction, and the queen followed Letty to the guest bedrooms silently.

Letty and Jocelyn had decided to put the king and queen in the middle bedroom, with the prince in the bedroom closest to the stairs. Their servant would be staying in the room on the opposite side—the only room without a painting on the wall.

"I'll make sure your trunk is brought to the correct room," Letty cheerily assured the queen when they arrived at the room. "Is there anything else you need? Anything I can get for you?" Letty asked.

"No, thank you. You may go." Queen Adelaide's tone reminded Letty of the way Princess Maisy had spoken to her when she first arrived at the castle: cold, commanding, and hardly seeming to notice Letty at all.

Letty gave the queen an awkward, shallow curtsy, then went back down to the grand entry to direct the footmen where the trunks should go when they were brought in.

There were still a few minutes until luncheon after Letty finished that task. She considered stopping by the kitchen to see if she could be of help there, or perhaps she would venture into the gardens to check on the prince and princess. Before she made her decision, though, Letty remembered that she had not put away the map she and Princess Maisy were looking at before the prince and his family arrived.

King Henrick and King Dorian will go through the library on their tour, Letty realized. *I've got to go clean up.* She scurried back to the library before the two kings could come down from the third floor.

What Letty didn't consider was how difficult it would be to roll and tie a map with only one hand available—far more arduous than it had been to lay it out. With her right arm in its sling, Letty had to awkwardly turn her wrist over itself in an attempt to roll the map up as it had been before. She pinned the loose edge down with her slung elbow while she slowly and carefully worked with the opposite end, ensuring that the edges lined up properly. At last she managed to shape the map back into a nice tube. Now the challenge was to wrap and tie the twine around it, which seemed nearly impossible. Letty poured every ounce of concentration she had into first looping the twine around the map, then into manipulating one end of the twine into a loop and using two fingers to wrap the other end around until she finally had a bow—certainly not a pretty one, but a bow, nonetheless.

Letty placed the map back atop the stack on the shelf and breathed a sigh of relief. The library was back as it should be, and she could avoid any trouble from leaving a mess while the Pelorian royalty were visiting. Satisfied, she started for the library door with the intention to go help in the kitchen, as she had thought to do before.

As she approached the door, she suddenly heard the voices of two men from the other side. *King Henrick and King Dorian*, Letty thought with dismay. She had hoped she would manage to leave the library before the two kings arrived. She quickly evaluated her options: she could stay put and simply explain that she was tidying up, or she could hide. A small part of Letty told her to just hold her ground; it shouldn't be the end of the world to run into the kings here. The much larger part of her, however, pulled her toward the bookshelves on the opposite side of the room. She ducked behind one of them, panicked, although she didn't quite know why. She forced herself to steady her breathing, closed her eyes, and hoped that King Henrick and King Dorian would not wander the rows of books.

"The library, unfortunately, is nothing exquisite." King Henrick's voice accompanied the slight groan of the door as it opened.

Letty scrunched up her nose and looked around, perplexed. She could hardly imagine anything more exquisite than this library, but she supposed the king had to be humble about the things he had.

"It's lovely," King Dorian replied dismissively. "But I'm still wondering what's below ground in this castle if you keep your armory on the third floor. Most I've seen keep their armories below ground."

"Storage space, mostly," King Henrick said, "and the rest is simply a dungeon."

This was a revelation to Letty. She hadn't even known that the castle had an official dungeon; she assumed, after what she had seen through the window, that it was all storage space.

"You are a brave man, keeping prisoners in your castle. Holding traitors and criminals in my own home is a risk I'm not willing to take," King Dorian replied.

"I'm not worried," King Henrick scoffed. "There are never many criminals down there. Of course, there are traitors, but not all of them are particularly dangerous."

"How in the world can there be a traitor who isn't dangerous?"

"Take the prisoner we arrested last week, for example. He had . . . certain information," King Henrick said slowly, "that he had no business knowing. That makes him a traitor. But he certainly isn't dangerous. I believe my sources told me he had a young family and worked as a tailor or cobbler or something of that sort. He wouldn't have the skills or the courage to make a plan that would put me in harm's way."

Letty's hand flew to her mouth. It was all she could do to keep herself from shouting. A cobbler in the dungeon who had been taken just last week? Perhaps it was just a coincidence, but it seemed far too strange to be *only* a coincidence.

The clock on the wall chimed twelve o'clock. "Luncheon will be served any moment now," King Henrick noted. "We'll finish the tour and our discussion after the meal."

Letty heard their footsteps leaving the library, and once the door closed, she peeked around the corner of the bookcase to make sure they were truly gone. The library was empty. Letty breathed a sigh of relief and flopped onto the floor. What in the world had King Henrick been talking about? Letty couldn't be sure, but it sounded suspicious, and she resolved then and there that she would get to the bottom of it.

CHAPTER 15

etty? Letty!" Letty snapped back to reality at the sound of Jocelyn's voice. They were sitting at the table in the kitchen, each with thick slices of bread and red strawberry jam in front of them. Well, Letty's was still in front of her, anyway; she suddenly realized that Jocelyn had already finished hers and was now staring at her, looking deeply concerned.

"Is something wrong?" Jocelyn asked. "You've been staring off into space for a few minutes now, and you haven't even touched your bread. What are you thinking about?"

"I'm sorry," Letty said bashfully. She took a bite of her bread and jam to give herself a moment to think before she spoke. She wanted to ask for Jocelyn's help learning more about the dungeon, but for some reason the question felt taboo. Before she could come up with a way to broach the topic, Jocelyn resumed the conversation she had been trying to have before.

"What do you think of the prince? The king and queen, too, of course, but especially the prince. I haven't seen any of them since I was a child, and I certainly never got to meet them." Jocelyn leaned against the table, eager to hear every detail Letty could offer.

"I'm not sure yet," Letty admitted. "I didn't spend much time with any of them. Queen Adelaide was very quiet when I brought her to her bedroom, but I haven't really spoken to anyone else."

"Oh, I see," Jocelyn replied. "Well, I suppose we'll just have to see over the next few days."

Letty nodded absently, not fully focused on the conversation at hand. Her eyes shifted from side to side, trying to determine if this was the right environment to discuss what she had heard in the library. No one seemed to be paying any attention to Letty and Jocelyn. Letty leaned in a bit across the table, and Jocelyn, sensing that Letty had something important to say, reciprocated.

"I overheard . . ." she started, then paused for a moment or two as she reconsidered her approach. "Do you know if the castle has some kind of dungeon?"

Jocelyn's eyebrows scrunched together. "Of course. What castle doesn't?" she replied.

"Are there actually prisoners there?"

Jocelyn's head tilted to the side and looked up for a moment as she thought. "I'm not sure, but I assume that there are sometimes. The guards would know if anyone is being kept there, I suppose."

"I'll have to talk to them, then," Letty said, looking around to see if any of the guards were eating nearby.

"Hold on, Letty, what is this about?" Jocelyn asked.

Letty hesitated. Her story was not certain, and it was very possible that Jocelyn would think she was crazy. Letty trusted Jocelyn, though, so with a deep breath, she launched in.

"I overheard King Henrick and King Dorian talking in the library—"

"You overheard what?" Jocelyn asked in shock. "How in the world did you manage that?"

"I was tidying up a map I left out in the library, and then they came in, and I panicked. I hid behind a bookcase," Letty admitted.

"Wow," said Jocelyn. "So you hid behind the bookcase. Go on, what were you saying you heard?"

"They were talking about dungeons and prisoners. King Henrick mentioned that there was a prisoner they brought in just last week for treason. He said the man was a tailor or a cobbler and had a young family."

"What does that mean?" Jocelyn asked, confused.

"Well, I've told you about Liam and Elsie, haven't I?"

"Yes, I think so. They're the children you love that live on your street, right?"

"Exactly," Letty confirmed, forcing her voice to remain quiet so as to not attract attention. "Their father is a cobbler, and when I went home last, I learned that he recently disappeared."

Jocelyn's eyebrows furrowed. "He just disappeared without a trace?"

"Yes. No one knows what happened to him."

"Wait. Are you telling me that you think this cobbler is sitting in the dungeon right now?"

"I can't be sure, but I think he might be."

"But, Letty, there are thousands of people in Trielle, and dozens of cobblers and tailors. It could be *anyone*, couldn't it?"

"I—I suppose . . ."

"And the king also said that the man was a traitor, didn't he? Has your cobbler committed treason?"

"I don't know," Letty said. "I can't imagine that he would have, but the king said it was something to do with some information. Maybe there was a misunderstanding of some kind."

"Listen, Letty," Jocelyn said, reaching across the table to take Letty's hand. "I know it might be easy to believe this is what happened to him when it's right in front of your face, but it isn't a good idea to go poking around a dungeon where you could run into dangerous people or get in trouble yourself."

Letty sighed. "You're right," she said.

But it didn't *feel* right. Something still seemed just a little bit odd. And what if Jocelyn was wrong? Letty knew Jocelyn was only trying to protect her, but Letty wouldn't be able to let go of the idea until she had done some investigating.

Jocelyn glanced over her shoulder at the clock on the wall. "You'd better hurry and finish that bread," she advised. "Luncheon will be over in two minutes."

Letty stuffed the rest of her food into her mouth as quickly as she could without choking.

"I'm going to help clean the dining hall when all the royals have finished. Do you want to join me?" Jocelyn asked when Letty had the last bite in her mouth.

Letty nodded as she swallowed. "Let's go," she said. She stood and started for the kitchen door that she always came through.

"This door, Letty," Jocelyn said. She pointed toward the other end of the kitchen. "This one leads straight to the dining hall."

Letty followed Jocelyn into the dining hall to begin tidying up from luncheon.

"Oh, I'm sorry, Your Highnesses," Jocelyn said as she and Letty entered. "I didn't realize you two were still here."

Princess Maisy and Prince Cassius stood at the end of the long dining table. It seemed they had just finished eating, and Letty assumed that Queen Adelaide and the two kings had just left.

"No, that's all right," Princess Maisy said, smiling. "Prince Cassius and I were just about to go to the ballroom so I could show him the piano piece I've been working on. Letty, I had been hoping to find you. Would you join us?"

"If you would like, I can come meet you when Jocelyn and I are finished cleaning up in here," Letty offered.

"Oh, no, please, go ahead, Letty. I don't mind at all," Jocelyn said.

"Are you sure?" Letty asked.

"Of course she's sure," Prince Cassius jumped in with a tone that somehow blended boredom and haughtiness. "After all, you are the princess's lady-in-waiting, not the maid's. Aren't you?"

Letty, Jocelyn, and Princess Maisy all stood for a moment in awkward silence, none of them sure how to answer the prince's snide comment.

"I'm sure, Letty. Go ahead," Jocelyn said at last.

"Wonderful! To the ballroom, then," said Princess Maisy.

Letty sent one more smile in Jocelyn's direction, then followed Princess Maisy and Prince Cassius to the ballroom.

"I have to admit, this new piece is still a work in progress, so forgive me if I miss a few notes," Princess Maisy said as she lifted the lid of the grand piano in the back corner of the ballroom.

"I will, don't worry," Prince Cassius assured her, poising himself on a seat nearest to the piano.

Princess Maisy sat down at the keyboard, took a deep breath, and began slowly plucking out notes. Her hands began to dance over the keys, the melody becoming faster and faster until, after a few moments, it became a fluid sound, moving and flowing with perfection. Letty had never heard this song before, but it was exceptionally beautiful. She had no idea Princess Maisy could play so well.

She clapped when the princess concluded her song—a soft, diminutive ending that put goosebumps on Letty's arms. "That was incredible, Your Highness," Letty said, noticing that the prince was not clapping.

"Yes, it was quite nice," Prince Cassius agreed, somewhat dismissively, while sitting stiffly in his chair. "I play, too, actually. I'll show you."

"Please do," Princess Maisy said. She stood and offered the stool to Prince Cassius.

Prince Cassius sat down, rubbed his hands together for a moment, and then dramatically began playing. His arms pumped up and down with his energy, and his face bore a haughty, aloof expression. Despite his countenance, his song was much simpler than the princess's had been and was riddled with errors. Letty and Princess Maisy smiled and nodded supportively as he played, enjoying the simple tune despite the occasional harsh note.

"Well done!" Princess Maisy said when he was finished, moving to stand beside him. "That's a wonderful beginning. May I give you a few pieces of advice that might make playing a bit easier?"

Prince Cassius cooly shrugged his shoulders. "I doubt it. I did notice that your fingers didn't look curved properly. Here, let me show you how to do it correctly," he insisted, gesturing for Princess Maisy to join him on the bench.

Letty raised one eyebrow and looked at Princess Maisy, but the princess graciously accepted the invitation and allowed Prince Cassius to show her how to curve her fingers—which, to Letty, looked exactly the same as what Princess Maisy had already been doing and seemed ridiculously unnecessary.

Letty watched for a while, but when it quickly became apparent that Princess Maisy wasn't going to play again, Letty started fidgeting a bit.

Princess Maisy turned over her shoulder, playing the mundane scales that Prince Cassius now had her practicing. "Letty, if you have other things you need to do, you can leave," she offered.

"Thank you, Your Highness. I'm going to see if Jocelyn needs any more help," Letty said quickly. "I'll meet you in the gardens as usual for tea." She started toward the doors out of the ballroom.

"She won't be having tea with us, will she? I don't understand why she was here to begin with," she heard Cassius murmur as she walked away.

Letty decided to pretend she hadn't heard that comment. After all, there was no reason to interrupt the courtship over a single statement. She heard Princess Maisy respond, but she couldn't hear the actual words the princess said.

Jocelyn was almost finished wiping down the dining table when Letty came back into the dining hall.

"Back so soon?" Jocelyn asked with a smile.

"After Prince Cassius decided that Princess Maisy needed lessons instead of them listening to each other play, there didn't seem to be much point in staying," Letty laughed. "I figured I would see if you needed any more help."

"I'm just about finished here," Jocelyn said. "It looks like you've got some free time until tea."

"All right. I'll see you later," Letty replied. She ducked back out of the dining room and into the grand entry.

She was about to go upstairs to read until teatime, but as she stood in the grand entry, one of the guards crossed her path. Letty made a split-second decision against Jocelyn's advice.

"Excuse me," she said. The guard turned around to face her. Letty recognized him. If she remembered correctly, she had heard Elias call him Clement at some point. "Your name is Clement, isn't it?" she confirmed.

"That's me," Clement replied. "Can I do something for you?"

"I had a question for you, actually," she said before she could talk herself out of it. "I was wondering if you could tell me anything about the prisoners in the dungeon right now."

Clement's demeanor instantly closed off. He crossed his arms over his chest and his eyes narrowed. "Now why would you ask a question like that?" he asked.

"Well, I . . . I was just curious . . ." Letty stuttered.

"Listen, I'm not supposed to be talking about that kind of thing, OK? I would recommend not poking around." His voice was stern and commanding. Letty's instinct was to back down, but his insistence only made her more curious.

"Why not?" she forced herself to ask.

"King's orders," Clement replied simply.

"I understand," Letty said. Clement nodded and turned to walk away. "I just have to ask," Letty continued to his back, "does one of them have light blue eyes and brown hair?"

Clement halted in his tracks.

"He has two toddlers and twin babies, and his poor wife is taking care of them all by herself with no idea where her husband is. Does that sound about right?"

"And how would I know any of that?" His back was still to Letty, as though he would walk away at any moment.

"I'm not saying you do," Letty reassured him. "I was just wondering if that sounds like it could describe a new prisoner."

Clement turned back around to face her. His face and eyes had softened, but his voice was still firm. "Like I said, I really can't be talking to you about this." His head swiveled around a bit, checking all around to make sure no one else was nearby, and then he lowered his voice. "But if you come to the entrance at 3:15, there might be a guard there who would help get your questions answered," he said.

Letty's eyes widened. "Where is the entrance?" she asked.

"There's a cellar door on the east side of the castle near the back. It leads down to the storage area, but that's where you can get to the dungeon too. But of course, you didn't hear anything from me," Clement said. He pulled his shoulders back, looked around one more time, and then walked back to the hallway that led to the kitchen.

A grin spread slowly across Letty's face. In less than two hours, she would see whether her suspicions were correct, and perhaps she could bring Kiana some valuable information about her husband. Then, maybe—just maybe—Liam and Elsie would somehow be able to get their pappy back.

CHAPTER 16

"Are you all right, Letty? You look a little flushed," Princess Maisy observed as Letty poured her tea at the little table in the gardens.

"Oh, I'm fine," Letty quickly responded. Truthfully, her heart was racing as she anticipated 3:15. It felt like the minutes were dragging on far longer than they should have been. She flashed a quick smile at the princess before turning to pour the prince's tea. "Cream and sugar?" she asked him cheerily.

"Sugar," he replied. Letty obliged and placed a sugar cube into his teacup. Prince Cassius looked up at her expectantly. "One more, if you please, girl," he said.

Letty felt a pinch in her chest at being called "girl" again. Her mouth opened to correct him, but immediately closed again. She would have to deal with the prince for only three days, and she couldn't risk upsetting him and ruining things for Princess Maisy. She simply dipped her head a bit and complied with his request.

"Actually, her name is Letty," Princess Maisy said kindly but firmly. She smiled up at Letty. "I'll have cream and sugar, please."

"Hmm," Prince Cassius replied as he sipped his tea. He didn't seem particularly concerned or interested.

Letty poured a generous amount of cream into the princess's tea and added one sugar cube, just as she knew Princess Maisy liked.

Thank you, she mouthed to the princess. Princess Maisy nodded in acknowledgment.

"Is there anything else I can do for Your Highnesses?" Letty asked when she finished serving them.

"I think that's all," Princess Maisy said, taking her teacup in her hand. "Prince Cassius, is there anything else you need?"

"No, she can be dismissed," he said with a pompous wave, eyes purposely avoiding Letty.

"All right, then, you can go do whatever you need until it's time to prepare for supper. Thank you, Letty," said Princess Maisy.

Letty curtsied and rushed away from the table. It was odd to not be having tea with the princess, but Letty was grateful she didn't have to sit there with Princess Maisy and Prince Cassius; she imagined it would have been extremely awkward. She was interested to hear what Princess Maisy would have to say about it at the end of the day.

Letty walked into the castle to check the time and see how long she would have to wait before going down to the dungeon. She eagerly looked at the first clock she could find: only 2:53. Twenty-two minutes left. It really wasn't a long time, but it felt like an eternity as Letty stared up at the clock. What would she do during that time?

After a moment's consideration, Letty decided to head back to the gardens. She would find the cellar door Clement had mentioned and make sure she knew where she was supposed to be, then figure it out from there.

Letty went around the opposite corner of the castle than she usually did. There was no need to check the areas she was already familiar with; she knew the entrance wasn't there.

It didn't take long for Letty to find the door in the ground. It was at an angle between the wall of the castle and the ground, just like other cellars. She couldn't see the prince and princess from where she was, but she knew they were somewhere around the corner and much farther back in the garden. Letty was a bit surprised that it wasn't better hidden, but Clement had told her it led down to the storage room first, not straight into the dungeon, so she supposed it made sense for the door to be easily seen.

With plenty of time to spare, Letty found a spot on the ground that was comfortable and within sight of the cellar door without being too close, just in case anyone walked by and became suspicious.

Once she settled in, Letty began imagining what she would find. She pictured a dank, dark room deep below ground, with Rylan the cobbler sitting frightened and alone against the wall. He would be shocked to see Letty, but she would figure out what was wrong and find a way to free him. Then she would bring him back to his family, and Liam and Elsie would rush to hug him while Kiana brought the babies to greet their pappy. Letty would watch from a distance, overjoyed at the reunion and satisfied with the role she had played in it. Yes, she could see it all perfectly.

Before she knew it, the sound of footsteps against the slightly crunchy grass alerted Letty that someone was coming toward her. She looked up with a start to see Clement approaching from the corner near the castle entrance.

Letty pressed her good hand against the ground, preparing to stand and meet Clement, but he shook his head sharply.

"Wait a minute," he instructed quietly as he got closer. "After I go in, another guard will come out. Wait until he's gone before you follow."

Letty nodded and backed away, allowing Clement to get to the cellar door while she did her best to look oblivious. She moved a bit farther from the door, making sure she could still see it, but trying to appear as though she hardly noticed the cellar door, much less cared about it. As hard as she tried, she couldn't keep herself from glancing every few seconds toward the door. Her fingers tapped rhythmically and impatiently against her leg as she waited. What was taking so long?

At last, after what was probably five or six minutes but felt like forever, the door opened again, and another guard emerged. He looked around as he rose from the opening in the ground and immediately spotted Letty. Letty felt her muscles begin to tense as he looked at her, and she had to make a conscious effort to keep her breathing relaxed. If this guard suspected that she had any intention of entering the dungeon when the king had instructed them to not even talk about it, he would certainly stop her, and she would probably be in trouble.

After examining her for a moment, however, the guard shrugged. He closed the door and strolled through the garden and around the corner at the front of the castle. Letty couldn't believe it. This was nothing short of a miracle. She waited a few more seconds to ensure that the guard was really gone, then rushed over to the angled door.

There were two halves of the door, each with a circular iron handle to open it. Letty grasped one of the handles with her good hand and pulled upward. The door was heavier than she had expected, and Letty strained to get it to move with only one hand. After a moment of effort, she let go and took a deep breath.

Please, she prayed, *I need to open this door. If Rylan the cobbler is down there, I need to find him.*

She took another deep breath, grabbed the handle firmly again, and pulled upward with all her might. Slowly, the door started to creak open inch by inch, until at last, the opening was wide enough for Letty to slip inside.

The door closed solidly above her head. This was it; she was in. No turning back now.

Directly beneath the cellar door was a staircase with wide steps, and Letty found herself on the top step. She took one creaky step down, then another and another down each of the ten steps until she reached the bottom, where she found a large storage area with crates and barrels stacked all around. Torches along the walls illuminated the space, and against the long wall, the flickering light showed Clement standing in front of a strong wooden door with a heavy lock.

"I'm impressed that you got that door open with only one arm," Clement said. "I can't let you stay long—I shouldn't be doing this to begin with."

Clement removed a large key ring from his belt and it tinkled noisily as he flicked through the keys until he found the one he was looking for. He inserted the key into the lock and turned. Letty's breath caught in her chest. *Here we go*, she thought.

"Only a few minutes," Clement reminded her. Letty nodded her understanding, and Clement pushed the dungeon door open just enough for her to pass through.

A small amount of sunlight filtered into the room through a little window high on the wall, hardly more than a slit. The only thing visible through it was a bit of sky, the green of some leaves, and one or two flower blooms.

The dungeon itself was cold and bare, with nothing on the walls and only thin cots on the floor. The furnishings of the room—or lack thereof—were the least interesting aspect, for sitting against the wall was exactly the man Letty had hoped she would find: Rylan the cobbler, blinking in surprise as Letty appeared in the doorway. What Letty hadn't expected, however, was the other man sitting next to him, with curly blond hair, green eyes, and scruffy facial hair that seemed to have been untouched for weeks. Letty froze in shock. After a moment, her brain finally began to process what she was seeing, and her eyes pooled with tears.

"Papa?"

1.0NSP422-157247 Printed in USA Jun-2024